New Zealand Travel Guide 2024

Your Ultimate Companion for Exploring the
Land of the Long White Cloud

Tony Mark

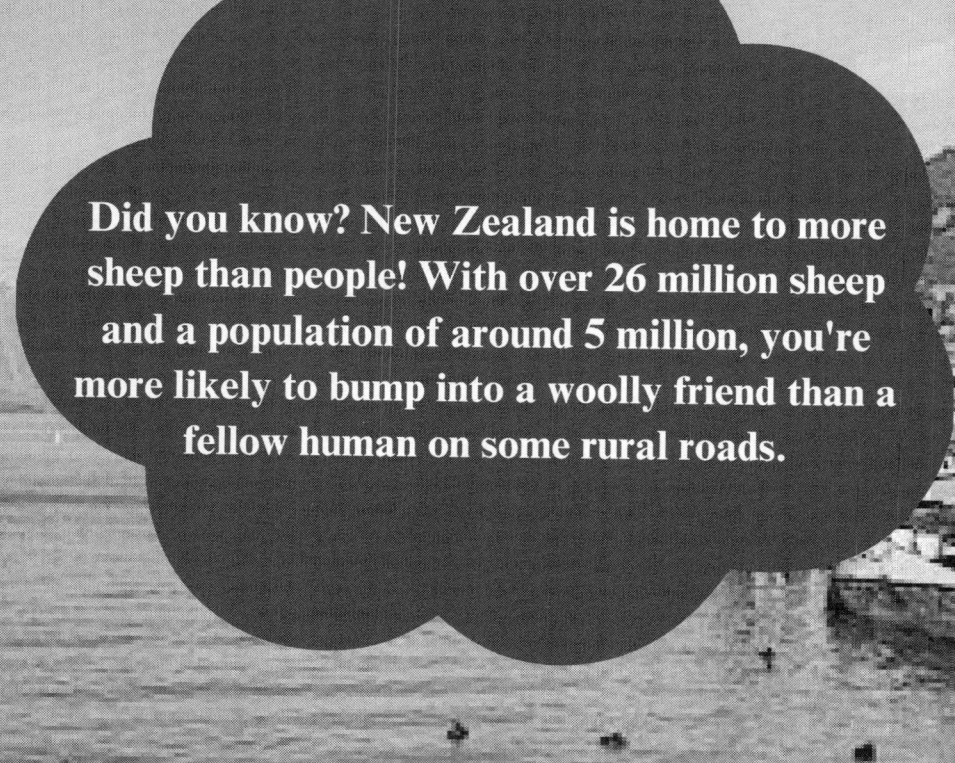

Did you know? New Zealand is home to more sheep than people! With over 26 million sheep and a population of around 5 million, you're more likely to bump into a woolly friend than a fellow human on some rural roads.

Copyright

All rights reserved. Before this document is duplicated or reproduced in any manner, the publisher's consent must be gained. Therefore, the contents within can neither be stored electronically, transferred, nor kept in a database. Neither in Part nor full can the document be copied, scanned, faxed, or retained without approval from the publisher or creator.

Copyright © Tony Mark, 2024.

Table of contents

Introduction — 1
- Welcome to Aotearoa
- Why New Zealand Should Be Your Next Adventure
- About This Guide
- A Brief Overview of New Zealand
- Essential Information for Travelers

Chapter 1 — 13
- When to Go
- Choosing Your Itinerary
- Types of Travel
- Budgeting for Your Trip
- Packing Essentials
- Responsible Travel in New Zealand

Chapter 2 — 39
- Top 10 Must-See Attractions and Hidden Gems
- Maori Culture
- Adventure Activities
- Natural Wonders
- Wine and Food
- Wildlife Encounters

Chapter 3 — 61
- **North Island**
- Bay of Islands
- Rotorua
- Taupo
- Wellington

- **South Island**
- Christchurch
- Abel Tasman National Park
- Queenstown
- Fiordland National Park
- Wanaka

Chapter 4 —————————— 93

- Getting Around New Zealand
- Accommodation
- Food and Drink
- Shopping
- Festivals and Events
- Language and Etiquette
- Health and Safety
- Staying Connected

Chapter 5 —————————— 125

- Useful Phrases in Te Reo Māori (Maori language)
- Packing Checklist
- Emergency Contacts
- New Zealand Travel Apps and Websites
- Maps (High-quality, detailed maps of North and South Island, major cities, and popular regions)

Auckland, New Zealand

SCAN THE QR CODE

1. open your device's camera app
2. point the camera at the QR code
3. Ensure the QR code is within the frame and well-lit
4. Wait for your device to recognize the QR code
5. Once recognized, tap on the map and input your current location for direction and distance to the destination

There is an entire section filled with maps for easy navigation

Introduction

"In the land where the mountains kiss the sky and the forests whisper ancient tales, adventure awaits."

Welcome to Aotearoa: The Land of the Long White Cloud

Welcome to Aotearoa, the Land of the Long White Cloud, a place where dreams take flight amidst a tapestry of breathtaking landscapes, ancient traditions, and adrenaline-pumping adventures.

New Zealand, a land of contrasts and captivating beauty, beckons explorers with its pristine beaches, towering mountains, verdant rainforests, and geothermal wonders.

From the dramatic fjords of Fiordland to the geothermal wonderland of Rotorua, from the sun-drenched vineyards of Marlborough to the snow-capped peaks of the Southern Alps, New Zealand offers an unparalleled diversity of experiences. Immerse yourself in the rich Maori culture, where ancient traditions and modern life intertwine seamlessly. Witness the mesmerizing haka, savor the unique flavors of a hangi feast, and learn about the legends and stories woven into the fabric of this land.

For the adventurous spirit, New Zealand is an outdoor playground like no other. Plunge into the heart-pounding thrill of bungy jumping, conquer towering peaks on epic hikes, or experience the rush of white-water rafting through pristine rivers. Embark on unforgettable wildlife encounters, where you might spot playful dolphins, majestic whales, or the elusive kiwi in its natural habitat.
Whether you seek tranquility amidst nature's splendor, an adrenaline-fueled escapade, or a cultural immersion into the heart of Maori heritage, New Zealand has something to ignite the soul of every traveler.

Let this guide be your compass as you navigate this extraordinary land, where every corner reveals a new wonder and every moment becomes an unforgettable memory.

Your adventure in the Land of the Long White Cloud awaits.

Why New Zealand Should Be Your Next Adventure

New Zealand isn't just another destination; it's a world of experiences waiting to be discovered. Here's why it's a must-visit for every type of traveler:

- **A Natural Wonderland:** New Zealand is nature's masterpiece. Picture dramatic fjords carving through ancient landscapes, pristine beaches with golden sands, lush rainforests teeming with life, and snow-capped peaks begging to be conquered. Every corner of this country offers a visual feast that will leave you breathless.
- **Adventure Awaits:** Whether you're an adrenaline junkie or prefer a more leisurely pace, New Zealand has an adventure for you. Bungy jump from dizzying heights, hike through breathtaking trails, cruise through tranquil waters, or cycle through picturesque vineyards. The options are endless!
- **Rich Cultural Heritage:** Immerse yourself in the unique Maori culture, where ancient traditions and modern life coexist harmoniously. Witness powerful haka performances, visit traditional marae (meeting houses), and learn about the deep connection between the Maori people and their land.

- **Warm Kiwi Hospitality:** Experience the genuine warmth and friendliness of the locals, known for their laid-back attitude and welcoming nature. You'll quickly feel at home as you engage in conversations, share stories, and create lasting connections with the people you meet.
- **Diverse Culinary Scene**: Indulge in a culinary journey like no other. Sample fresh seafood delicacies, savor world-class wines from renowned vineyards, and discover innovative dishes that blend international flavors with local ingredients. New Zealand's food scene is a reflection of its rich cultural heritage and abundant natural resources.
- **A Photographer's Paradise:** Capture postcard-perfect moments at every turn. From majestic mountain ranges to sparkling lakes, from vibrant cityscapes to tranquil rural scenes, New Zealand provides endless opportunities for stunning photography.

New Zealand is not just a destination; it's a journey of a lifetime. Let your senses be awakened, your spirit be invigorated, and your heart be captured by the magic of this extraordinary land.

About This Guide: How to Use It to Plan Your Dream Trip

This guide is your ultimate companion for unlocking the treasures of New Zealand, designed to empower you to plan and experience your dream adventure in the Land of the Long White Cloud. Whether you're an intrepid explorer seeking adrenaline-fueled thrills, a nature enthusiast yearning for serene landscapes, or a culture vulture eager to immerse yourself in Maori traditions, this guide has you covered.

How to Use This Guide:

- **Start with the Introduction**: Get acquainted with New Zealand's unique charm, diverse landscapes, and the essence of this guide.
- **Plan Your Adventure**: Chapter 1 equips you with essential planning tools, including the best time to visit, itinerary options, travel styles, budgeting tips, and packing essentials.
- **Discover Essential Experiences:** Chapter 2 unveils the must-see attractions, cultural encounters, adventure activities, natural wonders, wildlife encounters, and culinary delights that define New Zealand.
- **Explore Regional Guides**: Chapter 3 delves into specific regions and cities, offering detailed insights, recommendations, and practical tips for each area.
- **Navigate Practicalities**: Chapter 4 provides valuable advice on transportation, accommodation, food and drink, shopping, festivals, language, etiquette, health, safety, and staying connected.

New Zealand Travel Guide

- **Utilize Additional Resources:** Refer to the useful phrases in Te Reo Māori, packing checklists, emergency contacts, and recommended apps and websites for a seamless travel experience.
- **Delve into Special Sections:** Tailor your adventure with special sections dedicated to off-the-beaten-path experiences, family-friendly travel, romantic getaways, sustainable options, and road trip itineraries.

Navigating with Ease:
- **Maps:** Visualize your journey and plan your routes with detailed maps.
- **Highlighting and Note-Taking:** Personalize your guide by marking important sections and jotting down notes.

This guide is not just a book; it's your passport to an unforgettable New Zealand adventure. Use it as your trusted companion, and let it inspire you to create memories that will last a lifetime.

A Brief Overview of New Zealand: Geography, Climate, Culture, and Wildlife

Aotearoa, New Zealand, is a land of geographical marvels, diverse climates, a rich cultural tapestry, and fascinating wildlife:

Geography:
Comprising two main islands (North and South) and numerous smaller ones, New Zealand's landscape is a dramatic fusion of mountains, volcanoes, glaciers, fjords, and stunning coastlines. The North Island boasts geothermal activity, lush forests, and fertile plains, while the South Island is dominated by the majestic Southern Alps, creating a playground for outdoor enthusiasts.

Climate

Wildlife

Geography

Culture

New Zealand Travel Guide 7

Climate:

New Zealand enjoys a predominantly temperate climate, with warm summers and mild winters. However, variations exist across the country due to its latitudinal spread and diverse topography. The North Island experiences a subtropical climate in the far north, while the South Island's climate is more temperate, with cooler temperatures and higher rainfall in the west.

Culture:

New Zealand's culture is a unique blend of Maori heritage and European influences. The indigenous Maori people have a deep spiritual connection to the land, evident in their art, music, and traditions. Pākehā (New Zealanders of European descent) have also shaped the cultural landscape, contributing to a vibrant arts scene, a love for sports, and a strong sense of community.

Wildlife:

New Zealand's isolation has fostered a unique array of flora and fauna. The country is home to flightless birds like the iconic kiwi, the playful kea parrot, and the endangered kākāpō. Marine life thrives in the surrounding waters, with dolphins, whales, seals, and penguins frequently sighted.

Native forests shelter unique species like the tuatara, a living dinosaur, and the weta, a giant insect.

These features make New Zealand a truly unique destination, offering a wealth of experiences for every type of traveler. From the adrenaline-pumping adventures to serene landscapes, and from the vibrant cultural heritage to the fascinating wildlife encounters, New Zealand is a land of endless possibilities.

Essential Information for Travelers: Visas, Currency, Health & Safety, Transportation

Visas and Entry Requirements

Most visitors to New Zealand need a valid passport and either a New Zealand Electronic Travel Authority (NZeTA) or a visitor visa. The NZeTA is a digital travel authorization required for citizens of visa waiver countries staying for up to three months. If you're not eligible for an NZeTA or plan to stay longer, you'll need a visitor visa. Check your eligibility and apply for the NZeTA or visitor visa well in advance of your trip through the official Immigration New Zealand website: https://www.immigration.govt.nz/.

Currency and Money Matters

The official currency of New Zealand is the New Zealand dollar (NZD). Credit and debit cards are widely accepted in most establishments, and ATMs are readily available in cities and towns. It's advisable to carry some cash for smaller businesses or remote areas. Currency exchange can be done at banks, exchange bureaus, and some hotels. However, you'll likely get the best rates at exchange bureaus or by using your debit card at ATMs.

Tipping is not mandatory in New Zealand, but it's appreciated for good service. Rounding up the bill or leaving a small amount (5-10%) is customary in restaurants and bars.

Health and Safety

New Zealand has a high standard of healthcare, but it's recommended to have comprehensive travel insurance that covers medical expenses, including evacuation. No specific vaccinations are required for entry, but it's a good idea to be up-to-date on routine vaccinations like measles-mumps-rubella (MMR) and diphtheria-tetanus-pertussis (DTP).

Tap water is safe to drink throughout the country. However, if you're hiking or camping in remote areas, it's advisable to purify water from natural sources. New Zealand is generally a safe country, but petty theft can occur in tourist areas. Be mindful of your belongings and take precautions like using hotel safes.

Transportation
Getting Around New Zealand

- **Self-Drive:** Renting a car or campervan is a popular way to explore at your own pace. Remember that New Zealand drives on the left-hand side of the road.

- **Public Transportation**: Buses and trains connect major cities and towns. InterCity is the main national bus operator, while KiwiRail operates scenic train journeys.
- **Domestic Flights:** Air New Zealand and Jetstar offer domestic flights between major cities, saving time on longer journeys.
- **Ferries:** Regular ferry services operate between the North and South Islands, as well as to offshore islands like Stewart Island.
- **Cycling:** New Zealand has a growing network of cycle trails, offering a scenic and eco-friendly way to travel.
- **Walking:** Many towns and cities are pedestrian-friendly, and there are numerous walking tracks for exploring the natural beauty of the country.

Accommodation

New Zealand offers a wide range of accommodation options to suit every budget and preference, including:

- **Hotels and Motels:** Ranging from luxury to budget-friendly options.
- **Holiday Parks and Campgrounds:** Ideal for campervans, tents, and cabins.
- **Backpacker Hostels:** Affordable options for budget travelers.
- **Bed and Breakfasts (B&Bs):** Offering a more personal and homely experience.
- **Farm Stays:** Experience rural life and immerse yourself in local culture.
- **Luxury Lodges:** Indulge in top-notch service and stunning surroundings.

Other Essential Information

- **Language:** English is the official language, although you'll also hear Te Reo Māori spoken.

- **Electricity:** The standard voltage is 230V/50Hz, and the plug type is Type I (two flat pins and a grounding pin).
- **Time Zone:** New Zealand Standard Time (NZST) is 12 hours ahead of Coordinated Universal Time (UTC).
- **Emergency Services:** Dial 111 for police, fire, or ambulance services.
- **Tourist Information**: i-SITE visitor information centers are located throughout the country and offer maps, brochures, and advice.

Remember, this is just a general overview. It's essential to research specific requirements and recommendations based on your individual needs and planned activities. The rest of this guide will delve deeper into each of these topics, providing you with all the information you need for a safe, enjoyable, and unforgettable journey through New Zealand.

Chapter 1

Planning Your New Zealand Adventure

"Your journey of a thousand miles begins with a single step – and a well-crafted plan."

When to Go: A Season-by-Season Guide for the Best Experiences

New Zealand's diverse landscapes and temperate climate offer a wealth of activities and attractions throughout the year. Here's a breakdown of each season, their unique features, and the ideal experiences to enjoy:

Summer (December - February):
- **Characteristics**: Warm, sunny days with long daylight hours. The average temperature ranges from 20°C (68°F) to 25°C (77°F) in most areas. The peak season for tourism, with vibrant festivals and events taking place across the country.

Ideal Activities:

Beach hopping: Explore New Zealand's stunning coastlines, from the golden sands of Abel Tasman National Park to the rugged beauty of Piha Beach.
Water sports: Swim, surf, kayak, paddleboard, or try your hand at sailing.
Hiking and trekking: Traverse the Tongariro Alpine Crossing, hike the Milford Track, or explore other scenic trails.

- **Wine tasting:** Visit the vineyards of Marlborough, Hawke's Bay, or Central Otago and indulge in world-class wines.
- **Festivals and events:** Experience the vibrant summer atmosphere at events like the Rhythm and Vines music festival or the New Year's Eve celebrations in Queenstown.

Recommended Months: December to February for warm weather and outdoor activities.

Autumn (March - May):
Characteristics: Milder temperatures with crisp, sunny days and cooler nights. The landscape transforms with vibrant autumnal colors, especially in regions like Central Otago and Hawke's Bay.

New Zealand Travel Guide

Ideal Activities:
- **Hiking and trekking:** Enjoy pleasant temperatures and fewer crowds on the trails.
- **Scenic drives:** Admire the stunning autumn foliage along picturesque routes like the Crown Range Road or the Forgotten World Highway.
- **Wine tasting**: Experience the harvest season and taste the latest vintages.
- **Wildlife viewing:** Spot native birds like the kea and tui in their natural habitat.
- **Recommended Months**: March and April for comfortable weather and colorful scenery.

Winter (June - August):
- **Characteristics:** Cooler temperatures with snow on higher ground. The South Island transforms into a winter wonderland, perfect for snow sports enthusiasts. The North Island remains mild with occasional rain.

Ideal Activities:
- **Skiing and snowboarding:** Hit the slopes at popular resorts like Queenstown, Wanaka, and Mount Ruapehu.
- **Glacier hiking:** Explore the Franz Josef or Fox Glaciers on guided tours.
- **Whale watching:** Kaikoura is a prime spot to see giant sperm whales and other marine life.
- **Hot springs:** Relax in natural geothermal pools like those in Rotorua or Hanmer Springs.
- **Recommended Months**: July and August for snow sports and winter activities.

Spring (September - November):

- **Characteristics:** Temperatures gradually warm up, and flowers bloom across the country. Rainfall is common, but the landscapes are lush and vibrant.

Ideal Activities:

- **Hiking and trekking**: Enjoy the rejuvenated trails and milder weather.
- **Wildlife viewing:** Witness the birth of lambs and calves on farms, and spot native birds like the kiwi and kākāpō.
- **Kayaking and boating:** Explore the waterways as they come to life with new growth.
- **Gardens and flower festivals:** Visit stunning gardens like the Hamilton Gardens or attend the Ellerslie International Flower Show.
- **Recommended Months:** October and November for pleasant weather and blooming landscapes.

Shoulder Seasons (March-May & September-November):

- **Benefits:** Milder temperatures, fewer crowds, and often lower prices for accommodations and activities.
- **Consider:** Shoulder seasons offer a great compromise for those who want to avoid the peak season rush and enjoy pleasant weather.

Additional Considerations:

- **North vs. South Island:** The North Island generally has a warmer climate, while the South Island experiences cooler temperatures and more distinct seasons.
- **Regional Variations:** Weather patterns can vary significantly between regions, so be sure to check local forecasts before planning your activities.

New Zealand Travel Guide

- **Personal Preferences:** Ultimately, the best time to visit depends on your personal interests and desired experiences. Consider what activities you want to do and choose the season that aligns best with your preferences.

By understanding the unique characteristics of each season, you can tailor your itinerary to ensure a memorable and fulfilling experience in New Zealand. Whether you're seeking adventure, relaxation, cultural immersion, or a combination of all three, this diverse and beautiful country has something to offer every traveler throughout the year.

Choosing Your Itinerary: North Island, South Island, or Both?

New Zealand's two main islands offer distinct landscapes, experiences, and cultural attractions. Deciding whether to focus on one island or combine both depends on your interests, time constraints, and travel style. Here's a breakdown of the pros and cons of each option, along with sample itineraries to inspire your planning:

North Island:
Pros:
- **Maori Culture:** The North Island boasts a higher concentration of Maori cultural sites and experiences, including traditional marae (meeting houses), historical sites, and cultural performances.
- **Geothermal Wonders:** Explore geothermal parks with bubbling mud pools, erupting geysers, and hot springs. Rotorua is the epicenter of this geothermal activity.
- **Beaches and Coastline:** Enjoy warm-water beaches, subtropical forests, and diverse marine life in the Bay of Islands and Coromandel Peninsula.
- **Urban Delights:** Auckland, the largest city, offers a vibrant cultural scene, diverse cuisine, and a bustling waterfront. Wellington, the capital, is known for its arts, coffee culture, and craft beer.
- **Easier Access:** The North Island is generally more accessible for international flights and domestic transportation.

Cons:
- **Smaller Size:** The North Island is smaller than the South Island, so distances between destinations are shorter, offering less dramatic scenery.
- **Less Alpine Scenery:** While the North Island has beautiful mountains, it lacks the scale and grandeur of the Southern Alps.
- **Fewer Glaciers:** The North Island has no glaciers, unlike the South Island, which boasts several.

Sample Itineraries:
- One Week: Auckland - Bay of Islands - Rotorua - Taupo - Wellington

- **Two Weeks:** Auckland - Coromandel Peninsula - Rotorua - Taupo - Tongariro National Park - Napier - Wellington
- **Three Weeks**: Expand the two-week itinerary with additional destinations like Northland, Taranaki, or the East Cape.

South Island:
Pros:
- **Dramatic Landscapes:** The South Island is renowned for its stunning alpine scenery, including the Southern Alps, Fiordland National Park, and Aoraki/Mount Cook National Park.
- **Glaciers and Fjords:** Explore majestic glaciers like Franz Josef and Fox, and cruise through the dramatic Milford Sound or Doubtful Sound.
- **Adventure Activities:** Queenstown, the adventure capital, offers bungy jumping, white-water rafting, skydiving, and more.
- **Wildlife Encounters:** Spot penguins, seals, dolphins, and whales on various wildlife tours and cruises.

Cons:
- **Larger Size:** The South Island is larger than the North Island, meaning longer driving distances between destinations.
- **Cooler Climate:** The South Island generally has a cooler climate, especially in the mountains.
- **Fewer Maori Cultural Sites:** While there are important Maori sites in the South Island, they are less concentrated than in the North Island.

Sample Itineraries:
- **One Week:** Christchurch - Kaikoura - Nelson - Abel Tasman National Park
- **Two Weeks:** Christchurch - Arthur's Pass National Park - Franz Josef Glacier - Queenstown - Fiordland National Park

Three Weeks: Expand the two-week itinerary with additional destinations like Wanaka, Dunedin, or Stewart Island

Combining Both Islands:
Pros:

The Best of Both Worlds: Experience the diverse highlights of both islands, from cultural immersion to adventure activities and stunning landscapes.
Flexibility: Create an itinerary that suits your interests and time constraints, choosing the destinations and experiences that appeal to you most.

Cons:
More Travel Time: Combining both islands requires more travel time and potentially higher transportation costs.
More Planning: Coordinating flights, ferries, and accommodations between islands can be more complex.

Sample Itineraries:

Two Weeks: Auckland - Rotorua - Wellington - Picton (ferry) - Nelson - Abel Tasman National Park - Franz Josef Glacier - Queenstown

Three Weeks: Expand the two-week itinerary with additional destinations like the Bay of Islands, Tongariro National Park, Wanaka, or Dunedin.

Choosing the Right Option:
The best option for you depends on your priorities:

Limited Time (1-2 weeks): Focus on one island to maximize your experience and avoid rushing between destinations.
Maori Culture Enthusiasts: The North Island offers a more immersive cultural experience.
Adventure Seekers: The South Island is a haven for outdoor activities and dramatic landscapes.
Nature Lovers: Both islands offer incredible natural beauty, so choose based on your preferred landscapes and activities.
Combining Interests: If you have more time (3+ weeks) and want to experience the diversity of both islands, a combined itinerary is a great option.

No matter which island or combination you choose, New Zealand promises an unforgettable journey filled with natural wonders, cultural encounters, and unforgettable adventures.

New Zealand Travel Guide

Types of Travel: Self-Drive, Tours, Campervans, Public Transport, and more

New Zealand is a country that caters to a variety of travel styles, each offering a unique way to experience its natural beauty, cultural attractions, and adventurous spirit. Whether you crave the freedom of the open road, the convenience of guided tours, or the immersive experience of a campervan adventure, there's a perfect fit for your preferences. Let's explore the advantages and considerations of each travel style:

1. Self-Drive:

Embarking on a self-drive journey through New Zealand gives you the ultimate flexibility and independence to explore at your own pace. With well-maintained roads, stunning scenery, and numerous attractions along the way, it's a popular choice for those who want to discover hidden gems and create their own adventure.

Advantages:
- **Freedom and Flexibility:** Set your own itinerary, stop wherever you like, and change plans on a whim.
- **Scenic Routes:** Enjoy the freedom to choose your own path, taking detours to explore lesser-known spots and off-the-beaten-track attractions.
- **Privacy and Comfort:** Travel with your chosen companions in the comfort of your own vehicle.
- **Cost-Effective for Groups:** Sharing costs with travel companions can make self-drive a budget-friendly option.

Considerations:
- **Driving on the Left:** New Zealand drives on the left-hand side of the road, which might require some adjustment for visitors from countries that drive on the right.
- **Navigation:** Familiarize yourself with local driving rules and road signs. Consider using a GPS device or smartphone app for navigation.
- **Cost of Car Rental and Fuel:** Factor in the cost of renting a car or campervan, as well as fuel expenses, when budgeting for your trip.
- **Parking:** In busy tourist areas, parking can be limited and expensive. Research parking options in advance, especially in cities.

2. Tours:

Guided tours are a fantastic option for travelers who prefer a more organized and hassle-free experience. With a range of tours catering to different interests, budgets, and time frames, you can sit back, relax, and let the experts handle the logistics while you soak in the sights and sounds of New Zealand.

Advantages:
- **Convenience:** Tours handle transportation, accommodation, and often include activities and meals, taking the stress out of planning.
- **Expert Guidance**: Knowledgeable guides share insights into the history, culture, and natural wonders of the places you visit.
- **Social Interaction:** Meet fellow travelers from around the world and make new friends.
- **Access to Remote Areas:** Some tours offer access to remote or difficult-to-reach locations that might be challenging to explore independently.

Considerations:

Cost: Tours can be more expensive than other travel styles, especially if they include luxury accommodations and activities.

Limited Flexibility: Itineraries are often set, leaving little room for spontaneous detours or changes of plan.

Group Dynamics: You'll be traveling with a group, which might not suit those who prefer solitude.

3. Campervans:

Campervanning (or motorhoming) combines the freedom of self-drive with the convenience of having your accommodation on wheels. It's a popular choice for those who want to immerse themselves in nature, wake up to stunning views, and enjoy the flexibility of camping in various locations.

Advantages:

Flexibility and Freedom: Choose your own campsites and explore at your own pace.

Cost-Effective Accommodation: Campervans often include kitchen facilities, saving you money on dining out.

New Zealand Travel Guide

- **Unique Experience:** Sleep under the stars, wake up to breathtaking views, and enjoy the outdoors in a unique way.

Considerations:
- **Driving and Parking:** Campervans can be larger and more challenging to maneuver than cars, especially in narrow roads or crowded areas.
- **Campsite Availability:** Popular campsites can book up quickly, especially during peak season. Reserve your spots in advance.
- **Limited Facilities:** Campervans typically have basic amenities, so be prepared for a more rustic experience.

4. Public Transportation:

New Zealand has a reliable public transportation network, including buses, trains, and ferries. While it might not offer the same level of flexibility as self-drive or campervans, it's a convenient and affordable option for those who prefer not to drive or want to reduce their environmental impact.

Advantages:
- **Cost-Effective:** Public transportation is generally cheaper than renting a car or campervan.
- **Relaxation:** Sit back, enjoy the scenery, and let someone else do the driving.
- **Environmental Friendliness:** Reduce your carbon footprint by choosing public transportation.

Considerations:
- **Limited Flexibility:** Schedules and routes might not align with your desired itinerary.
- **Less Frequent Service:** In remote areas, public transportation might be less frequent or non-existent.

No matter which travel style you choose, New Zealand offers endless possibilities for exploration and adventure. By understanding the advantages and considerations of each option, you can create a personalized itinerary that suits your preferences and ensures an unforgettable journey through this breathtaking country.

Budgeting for Your Trip: Costs for Accommodation, Food, Activities, and Transportation

New Zealand can cater to a range of budgets, from backpackers seeking affordable adventures to luxury travelers indulging in high-end experiences. Understanding the costs associated with accommodation, food, activities, and transportation will help you plan a trip that fits your financial comfort zone.

Accommodation:
New Zealand offers a wide range of accommodation options to suit every budget and preference:

Budget:
- **Hostels:** Dorm beds start around NZ$25-40 per night, while private rooms range from NZ$50-100.
- **Campgrounds:** Powered sites for campervans or tents start from NZ$20-35 per night, while basic cabins can be found for NZ$60-120.
- **Holiday Parks:** These offer a mix of campsites, cabins, and sometimes motel units, with prices varying depending on the facilities and location.

Mid-Range:
- **Motels:** Comfortable and convenient, motels typically cost NZ$120-200 per night.

- **Bed & Breakfasts:** Offering a more personalized experience, B&Bs typically cost NZ$150-250 per night.
- **Apartments and Holiday Homes:** Ideal for families or groups, apartments and holiday homes can be rented for NZ$150-300 per night.

Luxury:
- **Boutique Hotels:** Stylish and unique, boutique hotels can cost NZ$250-500 per night.
- **Luxury Lodges:** Offering exclusive experiences and stunning locations, lodges can cost NZ$500-1000+ per night.

Tips for Budget-Conscious Travelers:
- **Book in Advance:** Especially during peak season, booking accommodation in advance can help you secure better rates.
- **Consider Shoulder Seasons:** Traveling during the shoulder seasons (spring and autumn) can often result in lower prices for accommodations.

- **Cook Your Own Meals**: Self-catering can significantly reduce your food expenses. Many hostels and campgrounds have kitchen facilities.
- **Look for Deals and Discounts:** Check websites like Bookme and GrabOne for discounted activities and attractions.
- **Utilize Public Transportation:** Buses and trains can be more affordable than renting a car, especially for solo travelers or couples.

Food:
- Food costs can vary depending on your dining choices and preferences:

Budget:
- **Supermarkets:** Stock up on groceries for self-catering or grab a quick lunch at the deli counter.
- **Food Markets:** Explore local markets for fresh produce, snacks, and street food.
- **Fish and Chip Shops:** Enjoy a classic Kiwi meal at a reasonable price.

Mid-Range:
- **Cafés:** Grab a coffee and pastry, or enjoy a light lunch.
- **Pubs and Bistros:** Many pubs offer affordable meals and a lively atmosphere.

Luxury:
- **Fine Dining Restaurants:** Indulge in award-winning cuisine and exquisite dining experiences.

Tips for Budget-Conscious Travelers:
- **Pack Snacks:** Bring snacks from home or stock up at local supermarkets to avoid impulse purchases.
- **Eat Like a Local:** Look for restaurants frequented by locals for authentic and affordable meals.
- **Take Advantage of Happy Hour:** Many bars and restaurants offer discounted drinks and appetizers during specific hours.

Activities:

New Zealand offers a wide range of activities, from free to expensive:

Free:
- **Hiking:** Explore New Zealand's numerous hiking trails and national parks.
- **Beaches:** Enjoy swimming, sunbathing, and picnicking at the beach.
- **Scenic Drives:** Admire the stunning scenery from the comfort of your car.

Mid-Range:
- **Museums and Art Galleries:** Many offer free or discounted admission.
- **Wine Tastings:** Sample local wines at vineyards for a reasonable price.
- **Guided Walks and Tours:** Learn about the history and culture of a region with a knowledgeable guide.

Luxury:
- **Adventure Activities:** Bungy jumping, skydiving, helicopter tours, and other adrenaline-pumping activities can be pricey.
- **Luxury Cruises:** Explore Fiordland or the Bay of Islands in style on a luxurious cruise.

Tips for Budget-Conscious Travelers:

Look for Free Activities: Many cities and towns offer free walking tours, outdoor concerts, and other cultural events.

Purchase Activity Passes: Consider purchasing an activity pass if you plan to do multiple activities, as they can offer savings.

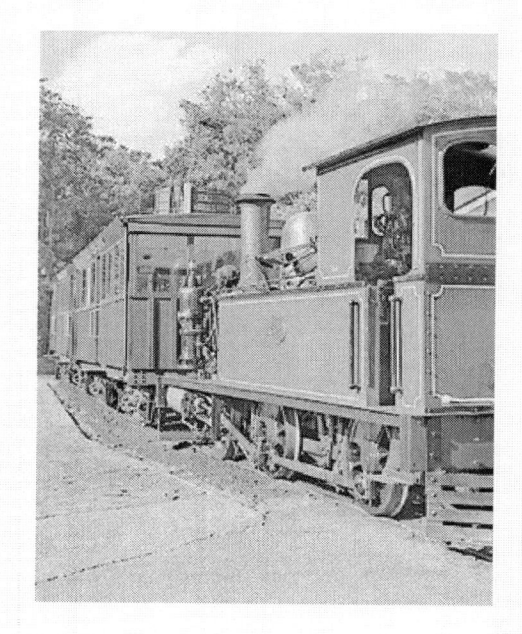

Transportation:

Transportation costs will depend on your chosen mode of travel:

Self-Drive:
- **Car Rental:** Rental rates vary depending on the vehicle type and season, but expect to pay around NZ$50-100 per day.
- **Fuel:** Petrol (gasoline) prices fluctuate, but budget around NZ$2.50 per liter.

Public Transportation:
- **Buses and Trains:** Prices vary depending on the distance and operator, but expect to pay around NZ$10-50 per journey.
- **Ferries:** Interisland ferry fares start from around NZ$50 per person.

Campervan Rental:
- Campervan rentals can range from NZ$50-200 per day, depending on the size and age of the vehicle.

Tips for Budget-Conscious Travelers:
- **Book Flights in Advance**: Securing flights early can often lead to lower fares.
- **Consider a Campervan Relocation:** Relocation deals offer significantly reduced rates for driving a campervan from one location to another.
- **Utilize Rideshare Apps:** If you're not renting a car, consider using ridesharing apps like Ola or Uber for short trips.

By understanding the costs involved and utilizing these tips, you can craft a New Zealand itinerary that fits your budget and allows you to experience the best this beautiful country has to offer.

Packing Essentials: What to Bring for Every Season and Activity

New Zealand's diverse climate and range of activities require thoughtful packing. Here are comprehensive packing lists tailored to different seasons and adventures:

Essentials for All Seasons:
- Passport and Visa (if required)
- Travel Insurance Documents
- Credit/Debit Cards and Cash
- Adapters and Converters: New Zealand uses Type I plugs (2 flat pins and a grounding pin).
- Medications and First Aid Kit
- Reusable Water Bottle
- Sunscreen and Sunglasses: Even in winter, the sun can be strong, especially at higher altitudes.
- Insect Repellent: Protect yourself from sandflies, particularly in warmer months.

- Travel Journal and Pen
- Camera or Smartphone
- Portable Charger

Clothing:

Base Layers: Merino wool or synthetic fabrics are ideal for moisture-wicking and warmth.

- **T-shirts/Shirts:** Pack a mix of short-sleeved and long-sleeved options.
- **Sweaters/Fleeces:** Choose versatile layers for warmth.
- **Jacket:** A waterproof and windproof jacket is essential year-round.
- **Pants:** Pack comfortable pants or shorts for warmer weather and hiking pants for outdoor activities.
- **Underwear and Socks:** Pack enough for your trip, considering laundry options.
- **Shoes:** Comfortable walking shoes or hiking boots, sandals or flip-flops for warmer weather.
- **Swimsuit (Optional):** If you plan on swimming or visiting hot springs.

Summer (December-February):
Additional Clothing:

- **Hat:** A wide-brimmed hat for sun protection.
- **Shorts:** Lightweight shorts for warm days.
- **Dresses or Skirts:** For a casual and comfortable option.

Additional Gear:

- Beach Towel: For swimming and sunbathing.
- Snorkel and Mask (Optional): If you plan to explore the underwater world.

Autumn (March-May):
Additional Clothing:
- **Light Scarf:** For added warmth on cooler evenings.

Additional Gear:
- **Waterproof Pants:** In case of rain.
- **Headlamp:** For hiking or exploring caves.

Winter (June-August):
Additional Clothing:
- **Thermal Underwear:** For extra warmth in cold weather.
- **Warm Hat and Gloves:** Essential for snow activities or chilly evenings.
- **Waterproof Pants:** To keep you dry in snowy or rainy conditions.

Additional Gear:
- **Snow Gear (if skiing or snowboarding):** Jacket, pants, goggles, and gloves.
- **Crampons (if glacier hiking):** For traction on ice.
- **Ice Axe (if glacier hiking):** For safety and balance.

Spring (September-November):
Additional Clothing:

Layers: Pack a variety of layers to adapt to changing temperatures.
Additional Gear:
Umbrella or Rain Jacket: For frequent spring showers.

New Zealand Travel Guide

Specific Activities:

Hiking:
- **Hiking Boots:** Choose sturdy boots with good ankle support.
- **Daypack:** Carry water, snacks, extra layers, and a first-aid kit.
- **Trekking Poles:** Optional, but helpful for steep or challenging terrain.

Water Sports:
- **Rash Guard or Wetsuit:** For protection from the sun and cold water.
- **Water Shoes:** For rocky beaches or water activities.

Camping:
- **Tent, Sleeping Bag, and Sleeping Pad:** Choose gear suitable for the season and expected temperatures.
- **Cooking Equipment:** If you plan on cooking your own meals.
- **Headlamp or Flashlight:** For navigating around the campsite at night.

Additional Tips:
- **Pack Light:** Avoid overpacking, as laundry facilities are readily available throughout New Zealand.
- **Check the Forecast:** Research the weather conditions for your destinations and pack accordingly.
- **Layer Up:** Dressing in layers allows you to adjust to varying temperatures throughout the day.
- **Choose Versatile Items:** Select clothing that can be mixed and matched to create different outfits.
- **Pack for Comfort:** Prioritize comfortable clothing and shoes, especially for long days of exploring.

Responsible Travel in New Zealand: Tips for Eco-Conscious Adventures

As you embark on your New Zealand adventure, embracing sustainable travel practices allows you to experience the country's natural beauty while minimizing your environmental impact and contributing to local communities. The Maori concept of "Tiaki" embodies the idea of guardianship and care for the land, people, and culture. By following the Tiaki Promise, you can ensure your journey is both fulfilling and responsible.

Minimize Your Environmental Footprint:
- **Reduce, Reuse, Recycle:** Follow the "3 Rs" by minimizing waste, reusing containers and bags, and recycling whenever possible. Look for accommodations and businesses that prioritize recycling and waste reduction.
- **Conserve Water:** Be mindful of water usage, especially in areas prone to drought. Take shorter showers, turn off taps when not in use, and report any leaks.
- **Choose Sustainable Transportation:** Opt for public transportation, cycling, or walking whenever possible. If renting a car, consider a fuel-efficient or electric vehicle. Explore the country's scenic train journeys for a unique and eco-friendly experience.
- **Support Eco-Friendly Accommodations:** Choose accommodations that have sustainable practices in place, such as energy-efficient lighting, water conservation measures, and recycling programs. Look for certifications like Qualmark's Enviro-Gold rating, which indicates a high level of environmental commitment.
- **Respect Wildlife and Natural Areas:** Observe wildlife from a distance, avoid disturbing their habitats, and follow guidelines for responsible wildlife viewing.

New Zealand Travel Guide

Stay on designated trails to protect fragile ecosystems, and avoid littering or leaving any trace of your visit.

Carbon Offsetting: Consider offsetting your carbon emissions from flights and other transportation by supporting reputable carbon offsetting projects.

Support Local Communities:

Shop Local: Purchase souvenirs and gifts from local artisans and businesses, supporting the local economy and preserving traditional crafts. Visit farmers' markets for fresh, locally-sourced produce and experience the vibrant community atmosphere.

Eat Local: Dine at restaurants and cafes that prioritize local ingredients and support sustainable farming practices. Try traditional Maori cuisine to immerse yourself in the local culture and flavors.

Stay Local: Choose accommodations that are locally owned and operated, contributing to the community's well-being. Consider staying at a marae (Maori meeting house) for a unique cultural experience and a deeper understanding of Maori traditions.

Volunteer: Participate in volunteer opportunities that contribute to conservation efforts, community projects, or cultural initiatives. This allows you to give back to the community and create a positive impact during your travels.

Learn About Local Culture: Engage with locals, learn about their history and traditions, and respect their customs and beliefs. Participate in cultural activities and events to gain a deeper appreciation for New Zealand's rich heritage.

Eco-Friendly Activities and Experiences:

- **Hiking and Biking:** Explore New Zealand's vast network of trails and cycle paths, immersing yourself in nature without leaving a carbon footprint.
- **Wildlife Conservation Tours:** Join guided tours that focus on responsible wildlife viewing and support conservation efforts.
- **Organic Farm Visits:** Learn about sustainable farming practices and sample fresh, organic produce.
- **Kayaking and Canoeing:** Paddle through pristine waterways, experiencing the tranquility of nature and observing wildlife from a respectful distance.

- **Glamping:** Enjoy the comforts of a luxurious camping experience while minimizing your environmental impact.
- **Visit Ecosanctuaries:** Explore protected areas where native species are thriving, contributing to conservation efforts.

By incorporating these sustainable practices into your travel plans, you can create a meaningful and responsible journey through New Zealand. Embrace the Tiaki Promise, tread lightly on the land, and leave a positive legacy for future generations to enjoy.

Chapter 2

Essential New Zealand Experiences

"Prepare to be awestruck. These are the moments that will define your New Zealand story."

Top 10 Must-See Attractions and Hidden Gems: A curated list of the most iconic and unique experiences

Embark on an unforgettable journey through New Zealand's iconic landscapes and hidden treasures. This handpicked selection of attractions showcases the country's natural wonders, cultural significance, and adrenaline-pumping adventures.

Milford Sound (Piopiotahi):
- **Location:** Fiordland National Park, South Island
- **Essence:** A breathtaking fiord where cascading waterfalls tumble down towering cliffs, creating a symphony of nature's power and beauty. Cruising through the mist-shrouded waters reveals dramatic peaks, lush rainforests, and playful marine life.

- **Significance:** Milford Sound is a UNESCO World Heritage site and a testament to the raw power of nature. It was carved by glaciers over millennia, resulting in a landscape of unparalleled grandeur.

Visitor Tips:
- Take a scenic boat cruise to fully appreciate the fiord's majestic scale.
- Hike the Milford Track, one of New Zealand's "Great Walks," for an immersive backcountry experience.
- Visit the underwater observatory to witness the unique marine life that thrives in the depths of the fiord.
- **Opening Hours:** Boat cruises operate year-round.
- **Admission Fees:** Vary depending on the cruise operator and duration.
- **Transportation Options:** Milford Sound is accessible by road (a scenic drive from Te Anau or Queenstown) or by air (scenic flights are available).

Tongariro National Park:
- **Location:** Central North Island
- **Essence**: A volcanic wonderland with three active volcanoes – Tongariro, Ngauruhoe, and Ruapehu – offering dramatic landscapes, challenging hikes, and unique geothermal features.
- **Significance:** Tongariro National Park is a dual World Heritage site, recognized for its cultural significance to the Maori people and its exceptional natural features.

Visitor Tips:
- Hike the Tongariro Alpine Crossing, a world-renowned one-day trek through otherworldly terrain.
- Ski or snowboard at Whakapapa or Turoa ski fields on Mount Ruapehu.

- Visit the Emerald Lakes, vibrant crater lakes with stunning turquoise water.
- **Opening Hours:** The park is open year-round.
- **Admission Fees:** There is no entrance fee for the park.
- **Transportation Options:** Accessible by car or shuttle bus from nearby towns like Taupo or Turangi.

Waitomo Glowworm Caves:
- **Location:** Waitomo, North Island
- **Essence:** Venture into a subterranean wonderland illuminated by thousands of glowworms, creating a mesmerizing spectacle of twinkling lights.
- **Significance:** The Waitomo Glowworm Caves are home to the Arachnocampa luminosa, a unique species of glowworm found only in New Zealand.

Visitor Tips:
- Take a guided tour to learn about the caves' geology and the life cycle of the glowworms.
- Opt for a boat ride through the Glowworm Grotto for a magical experience.
- Combine your visit with other activities like black water rafting or abseiling for an extra dose of adventure.
- **Opening Hours:** 9:00 AM to 5:00 PM daily.
- **Admission Fees:** Vary depending on the tour type and duration.
- **Transportation Options:** Accessible by car or shuttle bus from nearby towns like Rotorua or Hamilton.

Abel Tasman National Park:
- **Location:** Northwestern tip of the South Island
- **Essence:** A coastal paradise with golden beaches, crystal-clear waters, lush forests, and abundant wildlife. Explore by kayak, boat, or on foot along the Abel Tasman Coast Track.

Significance: Abel Tasman National Park is known for its diverse ecosystems, including unique plant species and marine life.

Visitor Tips:
Hike the Abel Tasman Coast Track, a multi-day trek with stunning coastal views.
Kayak through the turquoise waters and explore hidden coves.

- Take a boat trip to observe seals, dolphins, and other marine life.
- **Opening Hours:** The park is open year-round.
- **Admission Fees:** There is no entrance fee for the park.
- **Transportation Options:** Accessible by car, water taxi, or scenic flights from Nelson.

Please let me know if you would like more details for the remaining destinations or have any other requests!

Maori Culture: Understanding the indigenous heritage through marae visits, cultural performances, and historical sites

Maori culture is the beating heart of New Zealand, a living testament to the country's indigenous heritage and a vital thread woven into the fabric of its national identity. It's a culture steeped in history, tradition, and a deep spiritual connection to the land, known as "whenua."

Understanding and experiencing Maori culture is essential for any visitor seeking a truly authentic New Zealand adventure.

The Significance of Maori Culture:

- **Tangata Whenua (People of the Land):** The Maori are the tangata whenua, the indigenous people of New Zealand. Their ancestors arrived in Aotearoa over a thousand years ago, establishing a unique culture and way of life that has shaped the country's identity.
- **Te Reo Māori (The Maori Language):** Te Reo Māori is an official language of New Zealand, alongside English. Learning a few basic phrases not only shows respect but also opens doors to deeper cultural understanding.
- **Kaitiakitanga (Guardianship):** The Maori concept of kaitiakitanga emphasizes the responsibility to protect and nurture the environment. This philosophy is increasingly relevant in today's world and resonates with travelers seeking sustainable and responsible tourism.
- **Tikanga (Customs and Protocols):** Maori society is governed by tikanga, a set of customs, protocols, and values that guide interactions with others and the environment. Learning about tikanga helps visitors navigate cultural exchanges with respect and understanding.
- **Arts and Performance:** Maori arts and performance are renowned for their beauty, power, and storytelling. From intricate wood carvings and woven textiles to the mesmerizing haka (war dance) and poignant waiata (songs), Maori arts provide a window into the soul of the culture.

Experiencing Maori Culture:

- **Visit a Marae:** A marae is a communal meeting house that serves as the heart of Maori communities. Visiting a marae is a privilege and an opportunity to learn about Maori protocols, hear stories from elders, and witness traditional ceremonies. Many marae offer guided tours and cultural experiences for visitors.
- **Attend Cultural Performances:** Maori cultural performances are a feast for the senses, showcasing traditional music, dance, and storytelling. Look for kapa haka groups performing at festivals, events, or cultural centers. These performances are a vibrant celebration of Maori heritage and a chance to witness the power and passion of Maori artistry.
- **Learn About Maori History and Traditions:** Many museums and cultural centers across New Zealand offer exhibits and programs dedicated to Maori history, art, and traditions. Take a guided tour to gain insights into the Maori world view, their connection to the land, and the challenges and triumphs they have faced throughout history.
- **Participate in a Hangi:** A hangi is a traditional Maori method of cooking food in an underground earth oven. It's a communal feast that brings people together to celebrate special occasions and share stories. If you have the opportunity to attend a hangi, you'll not only experience delicious food but also a unique cultural exchange.
- **Learn Te Reo Māori:** Take a language course, attend a workshop, or use language learning apps to acquire basic phrases and greetings. Even a small effort to learn the language demonstrates respect and appreciation for Maori culture.
- **Visit Historical Sites:** Explore significant Maori sites like Waitangi Treaty Grounds, the birthplace of New Zealand's founding document, or Te Papa Tongarewa Museum of New Zealand, which houses a vast collection of Maori artifacts and taonga (treasures).

- **Connect with Maori Guides and Artists:** Seek out Maori-owned and operated businesses, art galleries, and cultural experiences. Engaging with Maori guides and artists provides a more authentic and meaningful understanding of their culture.
- **Participate in Workshops and Activities:** Many Maori cultural centers offer workshops where you can learn traditional crafts like weaving, carving, or ta moko (tattooing). These hands-on experiences provide a deeper appreciation for Maori artistry and skills.

By embracing the opportunity to learn about and experience Maori culture, you'll enrich your New Zealand journey and gain a profound appreciation for the country's unique heritage. The Maori people's warmth, hospitality, and deep connection to the land will leave a lasting impression and inspire you to connect with the natural world and each other in a more meaningful way.

Adventure Activities: Bungy jumping, skydiving, white-water rafting, hiking, and more for adrenaline junkies

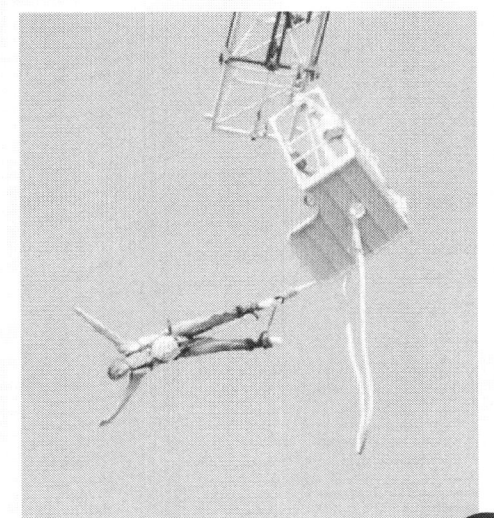

New Zealand's diverse landscapes, from rugged mountains to pristine rivers and dramatic coastlines, provide the perfect backdrop for an array of adrenaline-pumping adventures. Whether you're a seasoned thrill-seeker or a first-time adventurer, New Zealand offers experiences that will push your limits and leave you with unforgettable memories.

Bungy Jumping:

New Zealand is the birthplace of bungy jumping, and it continues to be a mecca for those seeking the ultimate thrill. Leap from towering platforms, bridges, or cliffs, and feel the rush of freefall before the bungy cord rebounds, sending you soaring back up.

- **Queenstown:** Home to the world's first commercial bungy jump site, the Kawarau Bridge Bungy, operated by AJ Hackett Bungy. You can also try the Nevis Bungy, the highest in New Zealand at 134 meters.
- **Taupo:** Experience the thrill of the Taupo Bungy, a 47-meter jump overlooking the Waikato River.
- **Auckland:** Take the plunge from the Auckland Harbour Bridge with AJ Hackett Bungy.
- **Safety Precautions:** Bungy jumping operators adhere to strict safety standards, including equipment checks, experienced jumpmasters, and medical assessments.
- **Recommended Operators:** AJ Hackett Bungy is a well-established and reputable operator with multiple locations across New Zealand.
- **Cost Considerations:** Bungy jumping prices typically range from NZ$150 to NZ$250, depending on the location and height of the jump.

Skydiving:

Experience the exhilarating sensation of freefall as you soar through the sky at speeds of up to 200 kilometers per hour. New Zealand offers stunning skydiving locations with breathtaking views of mountains, lakes, and coastlines.

- **Queenstown:** Skydive over the Remarkables mountain range and Lake Wakatipu for a truly unforgettable experience.
- **Taupo:** Take in panoramic views of Lake Taupo, Tongariro National Park, and the surrounding landscape.

- **Wanaka:** Skydive over the Southern Alps and pristine Lake Wanaka for a scenic adventure.
- **Safety Precautions:** Skydiving operators prioritize safety with comprehensive training, tandem jumps with experienced instructors, and high-quality equipment.
- **Recommended Operators:** NZone Skydive and Skydive Wanaka are reputable operators with excellent safety records.
- **Cost Considerations:** Skydiving prices vary depending on the altitude and optional extras like video footage. Expect to pay around NZ$300-500.

White-Water Rafting:

Paddle through exhilarating rapids, navigate through narrow canyons, and experience the thrill of conquering wild rivers. New Zealand's rivers offer a range of white-water rafting experiences, from gentle floats to adrenaline-pumping challenges.

- **Rotorua:** Raft the Kaituna River, home to the world's highest commercially rafted waterfall (7 meters), Tutea Falls.
- **Queenstown:** Tackle the Shotover or Kawarau Rivers for an action-packed adventure.
- **Rangitata River:** Challenge yourself with the Grade 5 rapids of the Rangitata River, known for its technical white water.
- **Safety Precautions:** Always choose a reputable rafting operator with experienced guides and safety equipment. Be sure to follow all safety instructions.
- **Recommended Operators:** Kaituna Cascades, Queenstown Rafting, and Rangitata Rafts are popular choices.
- **Cost Considerations:** White-water rafting prices range from NZ$100 to NZ$250, depending on the river and trip duration.

Hiking and Trekking:

New Zealand's diverse landscapes offer a wealth of hiking trails, from short walks to multi-day treks. Lace up your boots and explore lush rainforests, volcanic plateaus, alpine meadows, and coastal tracks.

- **Tongariro National Park:** Hike the Tongariro Alpine Crossing, a challenging but rewarding one-day trek through otherworldly volcanic terrain.
- **Fiordland National Park:** Tackle the Milford Track, a four-day hike through stunning scenery, including waterfalls, valleys, and rainforest.
- **Abel Tasman National Park:** Hike the Abel Tasman Coast Track, a multi-day coastal walk with golden beaches and turquoise waters.
- **Safety Precautions:** Be prepared for changing weather conditions, carry plenty of water and snacks, and tell someone your plans before heading out.
- **Cost Considerations:** Hiking is generally a free activity, but some multi-day treks require booking in advance and may have associated fees.

Mountain Biking:

New Zealand has a growing network of mountain bike trails, catering to all skill levels. From gentle family-friendly rides to challenging downhill tracks, you'll find the perfect trails to get your heart pumping and your adrenaline flowing.

- **Rotorua:** Home to the world-famous Redwoods Forest, offering a variety of trails for all abilities.
- **Queenstown:** Experience the thrill of downhill mountain biking at Skyline Gondola or explore the diverse trails in the surrounding hills.
- **Nelson:** Tackle the trails in the Codgers Mountain Bike Park or explore the scenic Great Taste Trail.
- **Safety Precautions:** Wear a helmet, use appropriate protective gear, and choose trails that match your skill level.

Other Adrenaline-Pumping Activities:

- **Canyoning:** Descend waterfalls, jump into pools, and explore hidden canyons in a thrilling adventure.
- **Ziplining:** Soar through the forest canopy on a zipline adventure, experiencing breathtaking views and an adrenaline rush.
- **Jet Boating:** Hold on tight as you jet boat through narrow canyons and experience 360-degree spins.
- **Cave Rafting:** Explore underground rivers and caverns on an inflatable raft.
- **Parasailing:** Get a bird's-eye view of the landscape as you soar high above the water.

Safety First:

Always prioritize safety when participating in adrenaline-pumping activities. Choose reputable operators with experienced guides, adhere to safety instructions, and wear appropriate safety gear.

Be aware of your own limitations and choose activities that match your fitness level and experience. By exploring the wide array of adrenaline-pumping activities available in New Zealand, you can create an unforgettable adventure that pushes your boundaries and leaves you with a newfound appreciation for the country's natural beauty.

Natural Wonders: Exploring glaciers, volcanoes, glowworm caves, fjords, and stunning coastlines

New Zealand, a land sculpted by geological forces over millennia, boasts a collection of awe-inspiring natural landscapes that captivate the senses and ignite the imagination. From towering glaciers to bubbling geothermal wonders, this country offers a diverse tapestry of geological formations, each with its own unique story to tell. Embark on a journey through these natural masterpieces and discover the breathtaking beauty that awaits.

Glaciers:
Franz Josef Glacier (Kā Roimata o Hine Hukatere):
Located on the West Coast of the South Island, Franz Josef Glacier descends from the Southern Alps to the rainforest below. Witness the raw power of nature as you hike to the glacier's terminal face, explore ice caves, or take a scenic helicopter flight for a bird's-eye view. Guided glacier hikes and ice climbing adventures offer a thrilling way to experience this dynamic landscape.

Tip: Book tours in advance, especially during peak season, and dress in warm, waterproof layers for unpredictable weather conditions.

Fox Glacier (Te Moeka o Tuawe):
Situated near Franz Josef Glacier, Fox Glacier is another awe-inspiring ice formation with its own unique features. Hike to the terminal face, take a helicopter tour, or embark on a guided ice climbing expedition.

Tip: Consider exploring both glaciers to compare their distinct characteristics and witness the ever-changing nature of ice formations.

Volcanoes:
Mount Tongariro:
Located in Tongariro National Park, Mount Tongariro is an active volcano with a rich cultural significance to the Maori people. Embark on the Tongariro Alpine Crossing, a world-renowned hike that traverses the volcano's diverse landscapes, including volcanic craters, emerald lakes, and steaming vents.

Tip: Check the weather conditions before embarking on the Tongariro Alpine Crossing, as it can change rapidly.

Mount Ngauruhoe:

Recognizable as Mount Doom in the Lord of the Rings films, Mount Ngauruhoe is an active cone volcano within Tongariro National Park. While climbing to the summit is challenging, the views from the top are rewarding, offering panoramic vistas of the surrounding volcanic landscape.

Tip: Obtain the necessary permits before attempting to climb Mount Ngauruhoe, and only do so if you are an experienced hiker with appropriate gear.

White Island (Whakaari):

An active marine volcano located off the Bay of Plenty coast, White Island is a unique geological wonder with bubbling mud pools, steaming fumaroles, and sulfur deposits. Take a guided tour to witness this otherworldly landscape and learn about its volcanic activity.

Tip: Due to the island's active volcanic status, access is restricted, and tours are subject to change or cancellation based on safety conditions.

Glowworm Caves:
Waitomo Glowworm Caves:

Descend into a subterranean world illuminated by thousands of glowworms, creating a mesmerizing spectacle of twinkling lights. Take a boat ride through the Glowworm Grotto, where the ceiling glows with the bioluminescence of these tiny creatures.

Tip: Maintain silence during the boat ride to avoid disturbing the glowworms and appreciate the tranquility of the experience.

Te Anau Glowworm Caves:
Located on the shores of Lake Te Anau, these caves offer a different glowworm experience, with a focus on the cave's geological formations and the life cycle of the glowworms.
Take a guided tour by boat and on foot, marveling at the cave's waterfalls, underground river, and the starry glowworm displays.
- **Tip:** Dress warmly, as the temperature inside the caves can be cool.

Fjords:
Milford Sound (Piopiotahi):
A majestic fiord carved by glaciers, Milford Sound is renowned for its towering cliffs, cascading waterfalls, and abundant wildlife.
Take a scenic boat cruise to fully appreciate the fiord's grandeur, or hike one of the many trails for panoramic views.
- **Tip:** Visit on a clear day to witness the full splendor of the waterfalls and surrounding mountains.

Doubtful Sound (Patea):
Larger and more remote than Milford Sound, Doubtful Sound offers a more secluded and tranquil experience.
Explore by boat or kayak, keeping an eye out for dolphins, penguins, and fur seals.
- **Tip:** Consider an overnight cruise to experience the fiord's serenity under the stars.

Other Unique Geological Formations:
- **Pancake Rocks (Punakaiki):** These limestone formations on the West Coast resemble stacks of pancakes, sculpted by the relentless forces of the sea. Witness the blowholes erupt as waves crash against the rocks.

Moeraki Boulders: Large spherical boulders scattered along Koekohe Beach on the South Island's east coast. These natural wonders have formed over millions of years and are shrouded in Maori legend.

By exploring these natural wonders responsibly and safely, you can contribute to their preservation and ensure their beauty remains for future generations to enjoy. Remember to respect the environment, follow guidelines, and choose reputable tour operators who prioritize sustainability.

Wildlife Encounters: Spotting kiwis, seals, dolphins, whales, penguins, and unique bird species

New Zealand's isolation and unique ecosystems have fostered a remarkable array of wildlife, from iconic flightless birds to playful marine mammals and intriguing reptiles. Embark on a wildlife adventure and discover the wonders of this natural kingdom, while adhering to responsible viewing practices to protect these precious creatures

Iconic Flightless Birds:
- **Kiwi:** The national symbol of New Zealand, the kiwi is a nocturnal, flightless bird with a long beak and bristly feathers. They are notoriously elusive but can be spotted on guided night tours at sanctuaries like Zealandia in Wellington, Rainbow Springs in Rotorua, or the West Coast Wildlife Centre.
- **Kākāpō:** The world's only flightless parrot, the kākāpō is critically endangered. Their unique breeding behavior and endearing personalities have made them a conservation icon. While sightings in the wild are rare, you can learn about their conservation efforts at sanctuaries like Zealandia or through documentaries.
- **Takahe:** Another flightless bird, the takahē was once thought to be extinct but was rediscovered in the Murchison Mountains in Fiordland National Park. Guided tours to the Murchison Mountains offer a chance to observe these striking birds in their natural habitat.

Playful Marine Mammals:
Dolphins:
- **Hector's Dolphins:** The world's smallest and rarest dolphins, found only in New Zealand waters. Encounter them on boat tours or kayaking trips in Akaroa Harbour, Marlborough Sounds, or off the coast of Kaikoura.
- **Dusky Dolphins:** Known for their acrobatic displays and playful nature. Swim with them on guided tours in Kaikoura or the Bay of Islands.

Whales:
- **Sperm Whales:** Kaikoura is a renowned whale-watching destination, where you can observe sperm whales year-round.

- **Humpback Whales:** These majestic creatures migrate through New Zealand waters during winter and spring. Spot them on whale-watching tours from Kaikoura, Auckland, or the Bay of Islands.
- **Orca (Killer Whales):** Occasionally spotted in New Zealand waters, particularly around the South Island. Join a responsible whale-watching tour for a chance to witness these apex predators.

Seals:

- **New Zealand Fur Seals:** These playful seals can be found basking on rocky shores around the country. Observe them from a distance in Kaikoura, the Catlins, or the Otago Peninsula.
- **New Zealand Sea Lions:** The world's rarest sea lions, found on the subantarctic islands and occasionally along the South Island's coastline. Join a guided tour to observe these magnificent creatures in their natural habitat.

Penguins:

- **Little Penguins (Blue Penguins):** The world's smallest penguins, found on various coastlines around New Zealand. Observe them returning to their nests at dusk in Oamaru, on the Otago Peninsula, or on Stewart Island.
- **Yellow-Eyed Penguins (Hoiho):** Endangered and found only in New Zealand, yellow-eyed penguins are shy and elusive. Join a guided tour on the Otago Peninsula for a chance to see these unique birds.

Other Fascinating Creatures:

- **Tuatara:** A living fossil and the only surviving member of its reptile order. See them at wildlife sanctuaries like Zealandia or on guided tours to the outlying islands.
-

- **Wetas:** Giant insects found only in New Zealand, with some species growing to the size of a mouse. Spot them on night walks in forests or on guided tours.
- **Long-Finned Eels:** Native to New Zealand, these eels can grow up to 2 meters long and live for over 100 years. Observe them in rivers, lakes, and estuaries.

Responsible Wildlife Viewing Practices:
- **Keep Your Distance:** Observe wildlife from afar to avoid disturbing their natural behavior.
- **Stay on Designated Paths:** Stick to designated trails and viewing platforms to protect fragile ecosystems.
- **Avoid Loud Noises and Sudden Movements:** These can frighten animals and disrupt their routines.
- **Never Feed Wildlife:** Feeding can alter natural behaviors and create dependence on humans.

Choose Reputable Tour Operators: Select operators who prioritize animal welfare and adhere to responsible wildlife viewing guidelines.

Wine and Food: Indulging in world-class wines, fresh seafood, farm-to-table cuisine, and Maori-inspired dishes

New Zealand's culinary scene is a vibrant tapestry woven from fresh, local ingredients, innovative techniques, and a deep respect for tradition. From world-renowned wine regions to bountiful seafood harvests, farm-to-table feasts, and the unique flavors of Maori cuisine, the country offers a diverse and delectable experience for every palate.

World-Class Wine Regions:
New Zealand has earned a global reputation for producing exceptional wines, particularly Sauvignon Blanc, Pinot Noir, and Chardonnay. Embark on a wine-tasting adventure through these renowned regions:

- **Marlborough:** The largest wine region in New Zealand, known for its crisp and zesty Sauvignon Blanc. Visit wineries like Cloudy Bay, Brancott Estate, or Wither Hills for cellar door tastings and vineyard tours.
- **Hawke's Bay:** Home to a diverse range of wines, including Merlot, Cabernet Sauvignon, and Syrah. Explore wineries like Te Mata Estate, Craggy Range, or Elephant Hill for a taste of this region's rich offerings.
- **Central Otago:** Renowned for its Pinot Noir, this region's cool climate and unique terroir produce elegant and complex wines. Visit wineries like Felton Road, Rippon Vineyard, or Amisfield for a taste of Central Otago's finest.

Fresh Seafood Delights:

Surrounded by the Pacific Ocean, New Zealand boasts an abundance of fresh seafood. Indulge in succulent delicacies like:

- **Green-Lipped Mussels:** These large, flavorful mussels are a New Zealand specialty. Try them steamed, grilled, or in a creamy chowder.
- **Bluff Oysters:** Prized for their creamy texture and briny flavor, Bluff oysters are a seasonal delicacy available from March to August.
- **Crayfish (Lobster):** Savor the sweet and tender meat of New Zealand crayfish, often served grilled or in a bisque.
- **Whitebait Fritters:** A delicacy made from tiny, translucent fish, whitebait fritters are a seasonal treat best enjoyed during spring.

Farm-to-Table Cuisine:

New Zealand's fertile land and passionate farmers provide a bounty of fresh, seasonal produce that chefs transform into innovative and delicious dishes. Seek out restaurants that champion local ingredients and sustainable practices, such as:

- **The French Café (Auckland):** A culinary institution renowned for its elegant French cuisine with a Kiwi twist.
- **Roots Restaurant (Christchurch):** Embraces seasonal ingredients and foraged flavors in its creative dishes.
- **Amisfield Bistro & Winery (Queenstown):** Experience farm-to-table dining with stunning views of Lake Hayes and the surrounding mountains.
- **The Kinloch Manor & Villas (Taupo):** This luxury lodge boasts a restaurant that showcases the best of local produce in a refined setting.

Maori-Inspired Dishes:
Immerse yourself in the unique flavors of Maori cuisine, which utilizes traditional cooking techniques and native ingredients. Try dishes like:
- **Hangi:** A feast cooked in an underground earth oven, featuring meats, vegetables, and seafood infused with smoky flavors.
- **Rewena Bread:** A sourdough bread made with fermented potato and flour, known for its tangy flavor and chewy texture.
- **Kawakawa:** A native plant used for its medicinal properties and unique peppery flavor, often brewed into tea or incorporated into desserts.

Food Markets and Culinary Experiences:
Explore vibrant food markets and culinary experiences to sample local delicacies, discover unique ingredients, and interact with passionate food producers:
- **Otago Farmers Market (Dunedin):** Held every Saturday morning, this bustling market offers a wide range of fresh produce, artisan cheeses, baked goods, and street food.
- **La Cigale French Market (Auckland)**: Immerse yourself in the flavors of France at this lively market, where you can find fresh pastries, cheeses, cured meats, and other gourmet treats.
- **Wellington Night Market:** Held on Friday and Saturday nights, this vibrant market offers a diverse array of international street food and local craft beer.
- **Cooking Classes:** Learn to prepare traditional Maori dishes or master the art of creating modern New Zealand cuisine with hands-on cooking classes offered throughout the country.

No matter where your culinary journey takes you in New Zealand, you're sure to find a wealth of delicious and unique experiences to satisfy your taste buds.

New Zealand Travel Guide

Chapter 3

Regional Guides

"From bustling cities to tranquil havens, each corner of New Zealand reveals its own unique charm."

North Island
Auckland: The City of Sails

Auckland, the largest city in New Zealand, is a vibrant and cosmopolitan hub with a rich history, diverse culture, and stunning natural beauty. Nestled between two harbors, the city offers a blend of urban sophistication and outdoor adventure, making it an ideal destination for all types of travelers.

History and Culture:
Auckland's history dates back to the 14th century when Maori settlers established villages in the area. European settlement began in the 19th century, and the city grew rapidly, becoming a major port and commercial center.

Today, Auckland is a multicultural melting pot, with a thriving arts scene, diverse cuisine, and a vibrant nightlife.

Must-See Sights:
- **Sky Tower:** Soaring 328 meters above the city, the Sky Tower offers panoramic views of Auckland and the surrounding region. Take a walk on the SkyWalk, an outdoor platform with no handrails, or try the SkyJump, a controlled base jump from 192 meters.
- **Auckland War Memorial Museum:** Housed in a grand neoclassical building, the museum showcases New Zealand's history, natural heritage, and Maori culture. Explore the extensive collections of artifacts, artworks, and interactive exhibits.
- **Auckland Art Gallery Toi o Tāmaki:** This modern art gallery houses a significant collection of New Zealand and international art. Admire works by renowned artists and discover emerging talents.
- **Waiheke Island:** A short ferry ride from Auckland, Waiheke Island is a haven for wine lovers, foodies, and beachgoers. Explore vineyards, sample award-winning wines, indulge in fresh seafood, and relax on pristine beaches.

Activities and Local Experiences:
- **Sailing:** Experience Auckland's "City of Sails" nickname by embarking on a sailing trip in the harbor. Take a guided tour or charter your own yacht for a personalized adventure.
- **Hiking:** Explore the lush rainforests of the Waitakere Ranges Regional Park or the volcanic cones of Mount Eden and One Tree Hill for breathtaking views of the city.

- **Food Markets:** Indulge in a culinary journey at La Cigale French Market, the Auckland Night Markets, or the Clevedon Farmers' Market, where you can sample local produce, artisan cheeses, and international cuisine.
- **Craft Beer Scene:** Discover Auckland's thriving craft beer scene by visiting local breweries like Brothers Beer, Hallertau Brewery, or Garage Project.

Off-the-Beaten-Path Suggestions:
- **Shakespear Regional Park:** Explore this stunning coastal park, home to beaches, walking trails, and a wildlife sanctuary.
- **West Coast Beaches:** Venture beyond Piha to discover lesser-known beaches like Karekare and Bethells Beach.
- **Tiritiri Matangi Island:** Take a ferry to this open sanctuary, where you can observe rare native birds like the takahe and saddleback.

Transportation:
- **Public Transportation:** Auckland has a comprehensive public transport network, including buses, trains, and ferries. Purchase an AT HOP card for convenient and discounted travel.
- **Taxis and Rideshare:** Taxis and ridesharing services like Uber are readily available.
- **Walking and Cycling:** Auckland is a walkable and cycle-friendly city, with dedicated bike lanes and shared paths.

Accommodation:
Auckland offers a diverse range of accommodations to suit all budgets and preferences, from luxury hotels to budget-friendly hostels and unique options like glamping or farm stays.

Dining:

Auckland's culinary scene is a melting pot of flavors, reflecting its multicultural population. You'll find everything from high-end restaurants serving innovative cuisine to casual cafes and ethnic eateries offering affordable meals. Be sure to try local specialties like whitebait fritters, green-lipped mussels, and hangi (traditional Maori feast). With its vibrant culture, stunning natural beauty, and endless activities, Auckland is a city that has something for everyone. Whether you're exploring the city's iconic landmarks, indulging in its culinary scene, or venturing into the surrounding natural landscapes, you're sure to create unforgettable memories in the City of Sails.

Bay of Islands: Subtropical paradise and historic sites

The Bay of Islands, a picturesque region in Northland, New Zealand, is a captivating blend of subtropical beauty and historical significance. With 144 islands scattered across sparkling waters, pristine beaches, lush forests, and charming towns, the Bay of Islands offers a diverse range of experiences for every type of traveler.

History and Culture:

The Bay of Islands holds a special place in New Zealand's history as the site of the country's first European settlement and the signing of the Treaty of Waitangi in 1840. The treaty, considered the founding document of New Zealand, established a partnership between the Maori and the British Crown. Today, the Bay of Islands is a living testament to this rich history and cultural heritage.

Must-See Sights:

- **Waitangi Treaty Grounds:** Explore the historic site where the Treaty of Waitangi was signed. Visit the Treaty House, the carved meeting house, and the Museum of Waitangi to learn about the treaty's significance and its impact on New Zealand's history.
- **Russell (Kororareka):** A charming seaside town with a colorful past. Stroll along the waterfront, visit historic buildings like Christ Church and Pompallier Mission, and enjoy the laid-back atmosphere.
- **Hole in the Rock (Motukokako Island):** Take a boat cruise to this iconic natural formation, a large hole eroded through a rock island. Keep an eye out for dolphins, whales, and other marine life along the way.
- **Urupukapuka Island:** The largest island in the Bay of Islands, Urupukapuka offers pristine beaches, walking tracks, and opportunities for camping and kayaking.

Activities and Local Experiences:

- **Dolphin Watching:** The Bay of Islands is home to a large population of bottlenose dolphins. Join a dolphin-watching tour for a chance to see these playful creatures up close.
- **Sailing and Boating:** Explore the islands and hidden coves by sailing boat, kayak, or stand-up paddleboard.

- **Fishing:** The Bay of Islands is a renowned fishing destination. Cast a line from shore or join a fishing charter to reel in snapper, kingfish, or marlin.
- **Hiking and Walking:** Discover the region's natural beauty on numerous walking tracks, including the Cape Brett Track, the Haruru Falls Track, and the Opua Forest Paihia Lookout Track.
- **Scuba Diving and Snorkeling:** Explore vibrant underwater ecosystems teeming with fish, coral, and other marine life.
- **Cultural Experiences**: Learn about Maori culture and history at local marae, museums, and cultural centers.

Off-the-Beaten-Path Suggestions:
- **Uretiti Beach:** A secluded beach known for its golden sand and clear waters. Ideal for swimming, sunbathing, and picnicking.
- **Aroha Island Ecological Centre:** Take a guided tour of this island sanctuary, home to kiwi birds, tuatara, and other native species.
- **Haruru Falls:** A picturesque waterfall surrounded by lush rainforest, offering a peaceful retreat from the crowds.

Transportation:
- **Car Rental:** A rental car is the most convenient way to explore the Bay of Islands at your own pace.
- **Buses:** InterCity and other bus companies operate services between major towns in the region.
- **Ferries:** Regular ferry services connect Paihia and Russell, as well as other islands in the bay.

Accommodation:
The Bay of Islands offers a wide range of accommodation options to suit every budget and preference, including hotels, motels, holiday parks, lodges, and apartments.

Dining:
Enjoy fresh seafood, local produce, and international cuisine at the many restaurants, cafes, and bars throughout the Bay of Islands. Some popular dining options include:

The Duke of Marlborough Hotel (Russell): New Zealand's oldest licensed hotel, serving classic pub fare with a waterfront view.
Charlotte's Kitchen (Paihia): A casual eatery with a focus on fresh, local seafood and vegetarian dishes.

- **The Gables Restaurant (Russell):** An upscale restaurant with a fine dining menu and stunning views of the bay. With its diverse attractions, stunning scenery, and rich history, the Bay of Islands is a must-visit destination on any New Zealand itinerary. Whether you're seeking adventure, relaxation, or cultural immersion, this subtropical paradise has something for everyone.

Rotorua: Geothermal wonders and Maori culture

Rotorua, a city nestled in the heart of New Zealand's North Island, is a captivating destination renowned for its geothermal activity and rich Maori heritage.

The city's unique landscape, shaped by volcanic forces, offers a surreal experience with its bubbling mud pools, erupting geysers, and steaming hot springs. Immerse yourself in the fascinating Maori culture, witness the power of nature, and indulge in a range of outdoor adventures.

History and Culture:
Rotorua's history is deeply intertwined with the Maori people, the tangata whenua (people of the land), who have inhabited the area for centuries. The city's geothermal features hold cultural significance, with many serving as sites for traditional rituals and practices. Rotorua is a hub for Maori arts, crafts, and performance, offering visitors a chance to experience the rich heritage and traditions of the indigenous people.

Must-See Sights:
- **Te Puia:** A geothermal valley and Maori cultural center where you can witness the impressive Pohutu Geyser erupt, explore bubbling mud pools, and learn about Maori art, carving, and weaving.
- **Whakarewarewa - The Living Maori Village:** Immerse yourself in a living Maori village, where you can observe traditional practices, learn about the geothermal landscape, and even taste food cooked in natural hot pools.
- **Waimangu Volcanic Valley:** Explore a geothermal wonderland created by the 1886 Mount Tarawera eruption. Walk through steaming volcanic craters, marvel at unique plant life, and witness the Frying Pan Lake, the world's largest hot spring.
- **Government Gardens:** Stroll through picturesque gardens, admire the historic Bath House (now the Rotorua Museum), and relax in the Polynesian Spa, a world-renowned geothermal bathing complex.

- **Redwoods Forest (Whakarewarewa Forest):** Hike or bike through towering redwood trees, explore a network of trails, and experience the tranquility of this unique forest environment.

Activities and Local Experiences:
- **Mountain Biking:** Rotorua boasts world-class mountain biking trails in the Redwoods Forest and other areas, catering to all skill levels.
- **Hiking:** Explore geothermal landscapes, native forests, and lakeshores on numerous hiking trails.
- **Agrodome Farm Show:** Witness sheep shearing, dog trials, and other agricultural demonstrations, and learn about New Zealand's farming heritage.
- **Zorbing:** Roll downhill inside a giant inflatable ball for a unique and exhilarating experience.
- **White-Water Rafting:** Tackle the rapids of the Kaituna River, including the world's highest commercially rafted waterfall, Tutea Falls.
- **Skyline Rotorua:** Ride a gondola for stunning views, try the Luge (a gravity-fueled cart ride), and experience the thrilling Skyswing.

Off-the-Beaten-Path Suggestions:
- **Kerosene Creek:** A natural hot stream where you can soak in warm geothermal waters surrounded by native bush.
- **Secret Spot Hot Tubs:** A hidden gem offering private hot tubs with stunning views of Lake Rotorua.
- **Kuirau Park:** A public park with geothermal features like mud pools and foot baths, perfect for a relaxing stroll.

Transportation:
- **Car Rental:** Renting a car is the most convenient way to explore Rotorua and its surrounding attractions.
- **Buses:** Local buses operate within Rotorua and connect to nearby towns.
- **Shuttle Buses:** Many tour operators offer shuttle services to and from attractions.
- **Taxis:** Taxis are readily available, but can be expensive for longer distances.

Accommodation:
Rotorua offers a diverse range of accommodation options to suit all budgets, including hotels, motels, holiday parks, lodges, and apartments.

Dining:
Rotorua's dining scene caters to all tastes, with options ranging from casual cafes and pubs to fine dining restaurants. Be sure to try local specialties like hangi (Maori feast), lamb dishes, and fresh seafood.

Rotorua is a destination that awakens the senses and leaves a lasting impression on all who visit. Whether you're captivated by its geothermal wonders, immersed in Maori culture, or seeking outdoor adventures, Rotorua offers a unique and unforgettable experience.

Taupo: Adventure capital and stunning lake scenery

Nestled on the shores of the magnificent Lake Taupo, New Zealand's largest lake, Taupo is a haven for outdoor enthusiasts and nature lovers. With its breathtaking scenery, adrenaline-pumping activities, and rich cultural heritage, Taupo offers a diverse range of experiences for every type of traveler.

History and Culture:
The Taupo region has a rich history dating back to the Maori people, who settled here over a thousand years ago. The lake itself is a caldera formed by a massive volcanic eruption around 26,500 years ago. Maori rock carvings on the cliffs of Mine Bay attest to the area's cultural significance. Today, Taupo is a thriving town with a strong connection to its Maori roots and a vibrant arts and crafts scene.

Must-See Sights:
- **Huka Falls:** Witness the raw power of nature as the Waikato River thunders through a narrow gorge, creating a spectacular waterfall. Take a walk along the viewing platforms or opt for a jet boat ride for a closer look.
- **Mine Bay Maori Rock Carvings:** Embark on a boat cruise or kayak trip to Mine Bay, where you'll see intricate Maori rock carvings depicting ancestral figures and mythical creatures.
- **Craters of the Moon:** Explore a geothermal park with steaming vents, bubbling mud pools, and colorful mineral deposits. Walk along the boardwalk trails and feel the heat beneath your feet.

- **Orakei Korako Cave and Thermal Park:** Discover a hidden gem with its unique silica terraces, geysers, and bubbling mud pools. Take a guided tour to learn about the geothermal activity and Maori legends associated with the area.
- **Taupo Bungy:** Leap from a platform 47 meters above the Waikato River for an adrenaline rush and stunning views of the surrounding landscape.

Activities and Local Experiences:
- **Skydiving:** Soar through the sky and experience the thrill of freefall with panoramic views of Lake Taupo and the volcanic peaks.
- **Bungy Jumping:** Take the plunge from the Taupo Bungy platform for a heart-pounding adventure.
- **White-Water Rafting:** Navigate the Tongariro River's rapids for an exciting water adventure.
- **Jet Boating:** Speed across Lake Taupo and experience 360-degree spins on a thrilling jet boat ride.
- **Fishing:** Taupo is renowned for its trout fishing. Cast a line from the shore, hire a boat, or join a guided fishing tour.
- **Hiking and Biking:** Explore the numerous trails around Lake Taupo, Tongariro National Park, and the surrounding hills.
- **Cruises and Kayaking:** Discover the lake's hidden bays and coves on a leisurely cruise or kayak trip.
- **Hot Springs:** Relax and rejuvenate in natural geothermal hot springs like Wairakei Terraces or DeBretts Hot Springs.

Off-the-Beaten-Path Suggestions:
- **Otumuheke Stream (Spa Thermal Park):** A free natural hot stream where you can soak in warm geothermal waters surrounded by native bush.

- **Aratiatia Rapids:** Witness the spectacular Aratiatia Rapids, created by the controlled release of water from a hydroelectric dam.
- **Huka Honey Hive:** Learn about honey production and sample a variety of delicious honey products.

Transportation:
- **Car Rental:** Renting a car is the most convenient way to explore the Taupo region at your own pace.
- **Buses:** InterCity and other bus companies operate services to and from Taupo.
- **Shuttle Buses**: Many tour operators offer shuttle services to and from activities and attractions.

Accommodation:
Taupo offers a wide range of accommodation options to suit every budget and preference, from campsites and holiday parks to motels, hotels, and luxury lodges.

Dining:
Taupo boasts a diverse culinary scene, with restaurants, cafes, and bars offering everything from casual meals to fine dining experiences. Be sure to try local specialties like trout, lamb dishes, and craft beers. With its abundance of outdoor adventures, stunning lake scenery, and rich cultural heritage, Taupo is a destination that offers something for everyone. Whether you're seeking adrenaline-pumping thrills, peaceful relaxation, or a taste of local culture, Taupo will leave you with unforgettable memories.

Wellington: The vibrant capital and cultural hub

Wellington, the vibrant capital city of New Zealand, is a captivating blend of cultural richness, culinary delights, and stunning natural beauty. Nestled between rolling hills and a sparkling harbor, this compact and walkable city offers a unique urban experience, where creativity, innovation, and a love for the outdoors thrive.

History and Culture:
Wellington's history dates back to the early 19th century when the first European settlers arrived. The city grew rapidly, becoming the political and cultural heart of New Zealand. Today, Wellington is a dynamic hub for arts, innovation, and sustainability. Its thriving arts scene is reflected in its numerous theaters, galleries, and festivals, while its culinary landscape boasts innovative restaurants and a flourishing café culture.

Must-See Sights:
Te Papa Tongarewa Museum of New Zealand: Immerse yourself in New Zealand's rich history, culture, and natural heritage at this world-class museum.

- Explore interactive exhibits, admire Maori artifacts, and discover the fascinating stories of this land.
- **Zealandia Ecosanctuary:** Step into a haven for native wildlife at this unique urban ecosanctuary. Take a guided tour to spot rare birds like the kiwi and tuatara, or explore the trails on your own.
- **Wellington Botanic Garden:** Escape the city bustle and wander through lush gardens, admire exotic plants, and enjoy panoramic views of the city and harbor.
- **Parliament Buildings (The Beehive):** Get a glimpse into New Zealand's political life by visiting the iconic Beehive, home to the country's parliament.
- **Mount Victoria Lookout:** Ascend to this hilltop lookout for sweeping views of Wellington, the harbor, and the surrounding landscape.

Activities and Local Experiences:
- **Cable Car:** Take a ride on the historic Wellington Cable Car, a funicular railway that offers stunning views as it climbs up to the Botanic Garden.
- **Cuba Street:** Explore this bohemian street, known for its eclectic shops, cafes, bars, and vibrant street art.
- **Weta Workshop:** Discover the magic behind The Lord of the Rings and other blockbuster films at this world-renowned special effects and prop studio. Take a guided tour or unleash your creativity in a workshop.
- **Craft Beer and Coffee Culture:** Sample Wellington's thriving craft beer scene at local breweries like Garage Project or enjoy a perfectly brewed cup of coffee at one of the many specialty cafes.
- **Wellington Waterfront:** Stroll along the waterfront promenade, admire the harbor views, and visit the City Gallery Wellington for contemporary art exhibitions.

Off-the-Beaten-Path Suggestions:

- **Breaker Bay:** Escape the crowds and head to this secluded beach, perfect for swimming, sunbathing, or simply enjoying the coastal views.
- **Red Rocks Reserve:** Embark on a scenic coastal walk through this reserve, known for its seal colony and dramatic rock formations.
- **Zealandia by Night Tour:** Experience the ecosanctuary after dark on a guided tour, where you might encounter nocturnal creatures like the kiwi and morepork (native owl).

Transportation:

- **Public Transportation:** Wellington has a well-connected public transport system, including buses and trains. The Metlink network offers various ticket options and convenient routes.
- **Walking:** Wellington is a compact city, and many attractions are within walking distance of each other.
- **Taxis and Rideshare:** Taxis and ridesharing services like Uber are available.

Accommodation:

Wellington offers a wide range of accommodation options to suit all budgets and preferences, from boutique hotels to serviced apartments and backpacker hostels.

Dining:

Wellington's culinary scene is a haven for food lovers, with diverse dining options ranging from fine dining establishments to casual cafes and international cuisine. Be sure to try local specialties like lamb, seafood, and craft beer.

With its vibrant arts scene, thriving culinary landscape, and stunning natural surroundings, Wellington is a city that effortlessly blends urban excitement with coastal charm. Whether you're exploring its cultural treasures, indulging in its culinary delights, or venturing into the surrounding wilderness, Wellington promises a memorable and enriching experience.

South Island
Christchurch: The Garden City and gateway to the South

Christchurch, the largest city on New Zealand's South Island, is a captivating blend of heritage, resilience, and natural beauty. Known for its expansive gardens, innovative architecture, and proximity to stunning landscapes, Christchurch offers a diverse range of experiences for visitors.

History and Culture:

Founded in 1850 by English settlers, Christchurch earned the moniker "Garden City" due to its numerous parks and meticulously manicured gardens. The city's history is marked by both triumphs and challenges, including devastating earthquakes in 2010 and 2011. Christchurch has since undergone a remarkable transformation, embracing innovative architecture and sustainable urban design while preserving its unique heritage.

Must-See Sights:

Christchurch Botanic Gardens: A sprawling oasis in the city center, home to diverse plant collections, tranquil walking paths, and the charming Avon River. Explore the rose garden, the native plant collection, and the conservatory.

- **Cardboard Cathedral (Transitional Cathedral):** A symbol of Christchurch's resilience, this innovative cathedral was built primarily from cardboard tubes after the original cathedral was damaged in the earthquake.
- **International Antarctic Centre:** Discover the wonders of Antarctica through interactive exhibits, a snow and ice experience, and encounters with Little Blue Penguins.
- **Canterbury Museum:** Delve into the region's natural history, Maori culture, and Antarctic exploration through fascinating exhibits and artifacts.
- **New Regent Street:** Stroll along this pedestrianized street lined with colorful Spanish Mission-style buildings, now home to boutique shops, cafes, and restaurants.

Activities and Local Experiences:

- **Punting on the Avon River:** Take a leisurely punting trip down the Avon River, gliding through the picturesque Botanic Gardens.
- **Street Art:** Discover the vibrant street art scene that has emerged in Christchurch since the earthquakes, adding color and creativity to the city.

- **Tram Ride:** Hop aboard the heritage tram for a nostalgic journey through the city center, passing by key landmarks and attractions.
- **Farmers Market:** Experience the local food scene at the Christchurch Farmers Market, held every Saturday morning, offering fresh produce, artisan foods, and crafts.
- **Adrenaline Forest:** Challenge yourself with a high ropes course set among towering trees, offering a thrilling adventure for all ages.

Off-the-Beaten-Path Suggestions:
- **Riccarton Bush:** Explore this remnant of native forest, home to diverse birdlife and walking trails.
- **Port Hills:** Hike or bike through the Port Hills for panoramic views of Christchurch, Lyttelton Harbour, and the surrounding landscape.
- **Little River:** Visit this charming village on the Banks Peninsula, known for its art galleries, craft shops, and scenic drives.

Transportation:
- **Public Bus:** Christchurch has a well-connected public bus network, operated by Metro.
- **Bike Share:** Explore the city on two wheels with the Nextbike bike-sharing system.
- **Taxis and Rideshare:** Taxis and ridesharing services like Uber are available.

Accommodation:
Christchurch offers a variety of accommodation options to suit all budgets and preferences, including hotels, motels, apartments, and backpacker hostels.

Dining:
Christchurch's culinary scene is thriving, with diverse dining options ranging from casual cafes and pubs to upscale restaurants. Be sure to try local specialties like lamb, seafood, and craft beer. Christchurch is a city that embodies resilience, creativity, and a deep appreciation for nature. Its vibrant cultural scene, stunning gardens, and proximity to diverse landscapes make it a must-visit destination on any South Island itinerary.

Abel Tasman National Park: Coastal walks and golden beaches

Abel Tasman National Park, nestled at the northern tip of New Zealand's South Island, is a coastal paradise renowned for its golden beaches, crystal-clear turquoise waters, lush native bush, and diverse wildlife. The park offers an idyllic setting for outdoor enthusiasts and nature lovers seeking tranquility and adventure.

History and Culture:
The park takes its name from the Dutch explorer Abel Janszoon Tasman, who first sighted the coast in 1642. The area has a rich Maori history, with evidence of early settlements and traditional use of the land for fishing and gathering resources. Today, the park is a protected area, managed by the Department of Conservation, ensuring the preservation of its natural and cultural heritage.

Must-See Sights:
Abel Tasman Coast Track: This world-famous 60 km track winds through lush coastal forest, offering breathtaking views of golden beaches, granite cliffs, and turquoise waters. The track can be completed in 3-5 days or tackled in shorter sections with water taxi access.

- **Split Apple Rock:** This iconic geological formation, shaped like a giant apple sliced in half, is a popular photo stop for boat tours and kayakers.
- **Cleopatra's Pool:** A natural rock pool with a smooth, water-worn slide, perfect for a refreshing dip on a warm day.
- **Bark Bay:** A picturesque bay with a long, sandy beach, ideal for swimming, sunbathing, and kayaking.
- **Tonga Island Marine Reserve:** A protected area teeming with marine life, offering opportunities for snorkeling and diving.

Activities and Local Experiences:
- **Hiking and Walking:** Choose from a variety of trails, ranging from short walks to multi-day hikes.
- **Kayaking and Canoeing:** Explore the coastline and secluded bays at your own pace.
- **Boat Cruises:** Take a scenic cruise to admire the park's coastline and spot marine wildlife.
- **Water Taxi Services:** Access different parts of the park and customize your itinerary with water taxi services.
- **Camping:** Spend a night under the stars at one of the park's Department of Conservation (DOC) campsites.
- **Swimming and Sunbathing:** Relax on golden beaches and take a dip in the clear waters.
- **Wildlife Viewing:** Look out for fur seals, little blue penguins, dolphins, and a variety of bird species.

Off-the-Beaten-Path Suggestions:
- **Pitt Head Loop Track:** A challenging hike with stunning views of the park's coastline.
- **Torrent Bay Estuary:** Explore this tranquil estuary by kayak or stand-up paddleboard.

Falls River Track: A scenic walk to a series of cascading waterfalls.

Transportation:
- **Car:** Drive to Marahau, the park's main entrance, from Nelson (1-hour drive) or Motueka (30-minute drive).
- **Bus:** Regular bus services operate between Nelson, Motueka, and Marahau.
- **Water Taxi:** Water taxis provide access to various points along the Abel Tasman Coast Track and offer scenic tours of the park.

Accommodation:
- **DOC Campsites:** Book in advance, especially during peak season.
- **Huts:** Basic accommodation options available for hikers on multi-day trips.
- **Lodges and Resorts:** Luxury options located outside the park boundaries.

Dining:
- **Cafes and Restaurants:** Limited options are available in Marahau and Kaiteriteri.
- **Pack Your Own Food:** Be self-sufficient for multi-day hikes.

Queenstown: Adventure playground and alpine scenery

Nestled on the shores of the crystal-clear Lake Wakatipu and surrounded by the majestic peaks of the Southern Alps, Queenstown is a haven for thrill-seekers and nature lovers alike. This vibrant town has earned its reputation as the adventure capital of the world, offering a plethora of adrenaline-pumping activities alongside breathtaking alpine scenery.

History and Culture:
Queenstown's origins trace back to the 1860s when gold was discovered in the Shotover River, attracting a wave of prospectors and adventurers. While the gold rush eventually faded, the town's adventurous spirit remained, evolving into a thriving hub for outdoor activities and tourism. Today, Queenstown embraces a lively atmosphere, welcoming visitors from around the world to experience its unique blend of adventure and natural beauty.

Must-See Sights and Activities:
- **Skyline Gondola and Luge:** Ascend to Bob's Peak on the Skyline Gondola for panoramic views of Queenstown, Lake Wakatipu, and the Remarkables mountain range. Then, race down the thrilling luge tracks for an adrenaline-fueled adventure.
- **Kawarau Bridge Bungy:** Experience the world's first commercial bungy jump at this iconic location. Leap from the bridge and freefall 43 meters towards the rushing Kawarau River below.
- **Shotover Jet:** Hold on tight as you jet boat through narrow canyons at high speeds, experiencing exhilarating 360-degree spins.

- **Skiing and Snowboarding:** During the winter months, Queenstown transforms into a winter wonderland, with world-class ski resorts like Coronet Peak and The Remarkables offering a variety of slopes for all levels.
- **Hiking and Biking:** Explore the stunning alpine scenery on foot or by bike, with trails ranging from easy walks to challenging multi-day treks. Popular options include the Ben Lomond Track, Queenstown Hill Time Walk, and the Tiki Trail.

Local Experiences:
- **Onsen Hot Pools:** Relax and rejuvenate in private hot pools overlooking the Shotover River Canyon.
- **Fergburger:** Indulge in a legendary Fergburger, a gourmet burger joint that has become a Queenstown institution.
- **Kiwi Birdlife Park:** Get up close to New Zealand's iconic kiwi bird and other native species in this wildlife sanctuary.
- **Arrowtown:** Step back in time to this charming gold rush town with its historic buildings, quaint shops, and scenic walks.

Off-the-Beaten-Path Suggestions:
- **Bob's Cove Track:** Hike this scenic track around Bob's Cove for stunning views of Lake Wakatipu and the surrounding mountains.
- **Moke Lake:** Escape the crowds and enjoy the tranquility of this secluded lake, perfect for kayaking, fishing, or simply relaxing by the water's edge.
- **The Remarkables Road:** Drive along this winding mountain road for breathtaking panoramic views of the Remarkables mountain range.

Transportation:
- **Queenstown Airport:** The airport is located just 10 minutes from the town center and offers domestic and international flights.
- **Shuttle Buses:** Numerous shuttle services operate between the airport, town center, and surrounding attractions.
- **Taxis and Rideshare:** Taxis and ridesharing services like Uber are available.

Accommodation:
Queenstown offers a diverse range of accommodation options to suit all budgets and preferences, from backpacker hostels to luxury hotels and apartments.

Dining:
Queenstown's culinary scene is thriving, with a wide variety of restaurants, cafes, and bars offering everything from casual meals to fine dining experiences. Be sure to try local specialties like lamb, seafood, and craft beer. Queenstown's unique blend of adventure, natural beauty, and vibrant culture makes it a destination that will leave you wanting more. Whether you're seeking adrenaline-fueled thrills, peaceful relaxation, or a taste of local life, Queenstown is sure to exceed your expectations.

Fiordland National Park: Dramatic fjords and untouched wilderness

Fiordland National Park, a UNESCO World Heritage site on New Zealand's South Island, is a testament to the raw power and beauty of nature. Carved by glaciers over millennia, this vast wilderness encompasses towering fjords, pristine lakes, ancient rainforests, and cascading waterfalls. It's a haven for outdoor enthusiasts, nature lovers, and those seeking solitude in a truly unspoiled environment.

History and Culture:
Fiordland's human history is relatively recent, with Maori people arriving in the area around the 13th century. They used the fiords for fishing and hunting, leaving behind rock art and other archaeological evidence of their presence. European explorers arrived in the 18th century, captivated by the region's dramatic landscapes. Today, the park is a protected wilderness area, offering visitors a chance to experience a landscape largely untouched by human development.

Must-See Sights and Activities:
- **Milford Sound (Piopiotahi):** The crown jewel of Fiordland, Milford Sound is a breathtaking fiord with towering cliffs, cascading waterfalls, and abundant wildlife. Take a scenic boat cruise or kayak through the fiord, hike to viewpoints like the Key Summit or Gertrude Saddle, or simply soak in the majestic scenery.
- **Doubtful Sound (Patea):** Larger and more remote than Milford Sound, Doubtful Sound offers a more secluded and tranquil experience. Explore by boat, kayak, or on a multi-day wilderness cruise.

New Zealand Travel Guide

- **Kepler Track:** A 60 km multi-day hike that circumnavigates the Kepler Mountains, offering stunning views of the Kepler Mire, Luxmore Cave, and Lake Manapouri.
- **Routeburn Track:** Another of New Zealand's "Great Walks," this 32 km track traverses the Southern Alps, offering breathtaking views of mountain peaks, valleys, and waterfalls.
- **Lake Te Anau:** The gateway to Fiordland National Park, Lake Te Anau is the second-largest lake in New Zealand and offers activities like boating, fishing, and kayaking.
- **Te Anau Glowworm Caves:** Take a boat trip to explore these mesmerizing caves, where thousands of glowworms create a magical spectacle of twinkling lights.
- **Wildlife Watching:** Look out for fur seals, penguins, dolphins, and a variety of bird species, including the rare and elusive kakapo.

Off-the-Beaten-Path Suggestions:
- **Dusky Sound:** The largest and most remote of Fiordland's sounds, Dusky Sound is a true wilderness experience, accessible only by boat or sea kayak.
- **Hollyford Track:** A challenging multi-day trek through the Hollyford Valley, offering a rugged and isolated backcountry adventure.
- **Lake Marian Track:** Hike to this alpine lake for stunning views of the Darran Mountains and a chance to see the endangered whio (blue duck).

Transportation:
- **Car:** The main access points to Fiordland National Park are Te Anau and Milford Sound, both accessible by road. Note that some roads may be unsealed or require a 4WD vehicle.

- **Bus:** Regular bus services operate between Te Anau, Queenstown, and Invercargill.
- **Boat:** Boat cruises are the primary way to explore the fiords, with various operators offering day trips and overnight cruises.

Accommodation:
- **Te Anau:** A wide range of accommodation options, including hotels, motels, holiday parks, and lodges.
- **Milford Sound:** Limited accommodation options, primarily lodges and campsites.
- **Doubtful Sound:** Overnight cruises are the main accommodation option.
- **DOC Huts:** Basic accommodation options available for hikers on multi-day treks.

Dining:
- **Te Anau:** A variety of restaurants, cafes, and pubs serving local cuisine and international fare.
- **Milford Sound:** Limited dining options, mainly focused on cafe-style meals and snacks.
- **Doubtful Sound:** Meals are included on overnight cruises.

Fiordland National Park is a truly remarkable destination, offering a pristine wilderness experience unlike any other. Whether you're exploring its dramatic fiords, hiking its rugged trails, or simply immersing yourself in the tranquility of nature, Fiordland is sure to leave a lasting impression.

Important Note: Fiordland's weather can be unpredictable, so it's essential to be prepared for all conditions. Pack warm and waterproof clothing, sturdy footwear, and a first-aid kit.

Wanaka: Lakeside charm and outdoor activities

Nestled on the shores of the picturesque Lake Wanaka, surrounded by snow-capped peaks and alpine meadows, Wanaka is a charming town that seamlessly blends relaxation and adventure. With its stunning scenery, vibrant arts scene, and abundance of outdoor activities, Wanaka is a must-visit destination for those seeking an authentic New Zealand experience.

History and Culture:

Wanaka's roots trace back to the 19th century when European settlers established sheep stations in the area. The town grew slowly, attracting farmers, adventurers, and artists drawn to its natural beauty and tranquility. Today, Wanaka retains its small-town charm while embracing a thriving tourism industry and a vibrant arts and culture scene.

Must-See Sights and Activities:

- **Lake Wanaka:** The centerpiece of the town, Lake Wanaka offers a myriad of activities, including swimming, kayaking, paddle boarding, boating, and fishing. Enjoy a leisurely stroll or bike ride along the lakeshore, or simply relax and soak in the stunning alpine views.
- **That Wanaka Tree:** This iconic willow tree, growing in the lake, has become a symbol of Wanaka and a popular photo spot. Capture its beauty at sunrise or sunset for a truly magical experience.
- **Mount Aspiring National Park:** A World Heritage Area, this park is a haven for hikers, climbers, and nature lovers. Hike to Rob Roy Glacier for stunning views of waterfalls and ice formations, or tackle the challenging Roy's Peak Track for panoramic vistas of Lake Wanaka and the surrounding mountains.

- **Puzzling World**: A quirky and interactive attraction featuring illusion rooms, a leaning tower, and a giant maze. A fun and unique experience for all ages.
- **Cinema Paradiso:** This charming movie theater with vintage couches and a classic car inside is a must-visit for film buffs. Enjoy a movie with a glass of local wine and homemade cookies.
- **Cardrona Alpine Resort:** During the winter months, Cardrona offers world-class skiing and snowboarding on its diverse slopes. In summer, enjoy activities like mountain carting, hiking, and scenic chairlift rides.

Local Experiences:
- **Wanaka Farmers Market:** Held every Thursday afternoon, this bustling market offers a wide range of fresh produce, artisan foods, crafts, and live music.
- **Rippon Vineyard & Winery:** Taste award-winning wines at this scenic vineyard, overlooking Lake Wanaka and the surrounding mountains.

- **Wildwire Wanaka:** Challenge yourself with a via ferrata (a climbing route with fixed cables) adventure, offering stunning views and adrenaline-pumping thrills.
- **Eco Wanaka Adventures:** Explore Lake Wanaka's hidden coves and islands on a guided kayak tour or eco-cruise.

Off-the-Beaten-Path Suggestions:
- **Mou Waho Island:** Take a boat trip to this predator-free island, home to rare native birds and a stunning crater lake.
- **Glendhu Bay Track**: Hike this scenic track around Glendhu Bay for panoramic views of the lake and mountains.
- **Diamond Lake and Rocky Mountain Track:** A challenging hike with rewarding views of the Southern Alps and surrounding landscapes.

Transportation:
- **Queenstown Airport:** Located about an hour's drive from Wanaka, Queenstown Airport is the closest international airport.
- **Shuttle Buses:** Regular shuttle services operate between Queenstown Airport and Wanaka.
- **Car Rental:** Renting a car is a convenient option for exploring the Wanaka region at your own pace.
- **Local Buses:** Limited bus services operate within Wanaka and to nearby towns.

Accommodation:
Wanaka offers a diverse range of accommodation options to suit all budgets and preferences, from backpacker hostels to luxury lodges and apartments.

Dining:
Wanaka's culinary scene is thriving, with numerous cafes, restaurants, and bars offering everything from casual meals to fine dining experiences. Be sure to try local specialties like lamb, salmon, and Central Otago Pinot Noir. Wanaka's laid-back charm, stunning alpine scenery, and abundance of outdoor activities make it a destination that will capture your heart and leave you wanting more.

Chapter 4

Practical Travel Tips

"Navigate the ins and outs of Kiwi life with these insider tips for a seamless and enjoyable journey."

Getting Around New Zealand: Transportation options and tips

New Zealand boasts a well-developed transportation network that makes exploring this breathtaking country a breeze. Whether you're embarking on a cross-country road trip, hopping between islands, or simply getting around town, various options are available to suit your needs and budget.

1. Self-Drive:
Renting a car or campervan is the most popular way to explore New Zealand, offering flexibility, freedom, and the opportunity to discover hidden gems at your own pace.

Car Rentals:

- **Companies:** Major international car rental companies like Hertz, Avis, Budget, and Thrifty, as well as local operators like Jucy and GO Rentals, offer a wide range of vehicles to suit different needs and budgets.
- **Booking:** Book your rental car in advance, especially during peak season (December-February), to secure the best rates and availability.
- **Requirements:** You'll need a valid driver's license from your home country or an International Driving Permit (IDP) if your license is not in English.
- **Insurance:** Comprehensive insurance is highly recommended to cover any unforeseen incidents or accidents.
- **Road Rules:** Remember that New Zealand drives on the left-hand side of the road. Familiarize yourself with local road rules and regulations before setting off.

Campervan Rentals:

- **Companies:** Several companies offer campervan rentals, including Maui, Britz, and Apollo. Choose from a variety of sizes and styles to suit your group size and budget.
- **Booking:** Book well in advance, especially if you're traveling during peak season or school holidays.
- **Facilities:** Campervans typically come equipped with sleeping areas, kitchenettes, and basic amenities. Consider your needs and preferences when choosing a model.
- **Campgrounds:** New Zealand has a network of holiday parks and campgrounds where you can park your campervan and access facilities like showers, toilets, and laundry.

Tips for Self-Drive:
- **Plan Your Route:** Research your desired destinations and plan your route in advance. Use online resources or GPS navigation apps to help you navigate.
- **Take Breaks:** New Zealand's roads can be winding and mountainous, so take regular breaks to rest and enjoy the scenery.
- **Fuel Up:** Petrol stations are widely available, but they can be less frequent in remote areas. Fill up your tank whenever you have the chance.
- **Safety First**: Always wear your seatbelt, drive defensively, and be aware of changing weather conditions.

2. Public Transportation:

New Zealand offers a comprehensive public transportation network, including buses, trains, and ferries, connecting major cities and towns throughout the country.

Buses:
- **InterCity:** The main national bus operator, InterCity, offers regular services between major cities and towns throughout New Zealand.
- **Regional Bus Companies:** Many smaller bus companies operate within specific regions, providing local connections and shorter routes.
- **Booking:** Book your tickets in advance online or at bus stations. Some operators offer discounts for booking online or purchasing multi-journey passes.

Trains:
- **KiwiRail:** The national railway operator, KiwiRail, offers scenic train journeys like the TranzAlpine (Christchurch to Greymouth) and the Northern Explorer (Auckland to Wellington).
- **Booking:** Book your tickets online or at train stations. KiwiRail often offers early bird discounts and special promotions.

Ferries:
- **Interislander:** Operates ferry services between the North and South Islands, connecting Wellington and Picton.
- **Bluebridge:** Another ferry operator offering crossings between the North and South Islands.
- **Booking:** Book your ferry tickets in advance, especially during peak season, to secure your preferred departure time and avoid disappointment.

Tips for Public Transportation:
- **Check Schedules:** Public transportation schedules can vary, so check timetables online or at stations to plan your journeys accordingly.
- **Consider Travel Passes:** If you plan to use public transportation extensively, consider purchasing a travel pass for discounted fares.
- **Luggage Restrictions**: Be aware of luggage restrictions on buses and trains, especially if you're traveling with large bags or bulky items.

3. Organized Tours:

Organized tours offer a convenient and hassle-free way to explore New Zealand, with various options catering to different interests, budgets, and time frames.

- **Bus Tours:** Explore specific regions or embark on multi-day journeys across the country with a comfortable coach and knowledgeable guide.
- **Small Group Tours:** Enjoy a more personalized experience with smaller groups and flexible itineraries.
- **Adventure Tours:** Experience adrenaline-pumping activities like bungy jumping, white-water rafting, or hiking with a guided tour.
- **Cultural Tours:** Immerse yourself in Maori culture and history with a guided tour that visits significant sites and shares local stories.

Tips for Organized Tours:
- **Research:** Choose a tour operator that specializes in your areas of interest and offers the type of experience you're looking for.
- **Read Reviews:** Check online reviews from previous travelers to gauge the quality and reputation of the tour operator.
- **Book Early:** Popular tours can book up quickly, especially during peak season, so reserve your spot in advance.

4. **Other Transportation Options:**
   - **Domestic Flights:** Air New Zealand and Jetstar offer domestic flights between major cities, saving time on longer journeys.
   - **Shuttle Services:** Many towns and attractions offer shuttle services for convenient transportation between destinations.
   - **Taxis:** Taxis are readily available in most towns and cities, but can be more expensive than other options.
   - **Rideshare:** Rideshare services like Uber are available in some areas, offering a convenient and sometimes more affordable alternative to taxis.

By understanding the various transportation options available in New Zealand, you can choose the best mode of travel for your itinerary and preferences. Whether you're exploring independently, joining a guided tour, or hopping on public transport, getting around New Zealand is an adventure in itself.

Accommodation: From luxury lodges to budget-friendly hostels and unique stays

New Zealand's accommodation landscape is as diverse as its natural beauty, offering a wide range of options to suit every budget, taste, and travel style. Whether you're seeking luxurious indulgence, budget-friendly comfort, or unique experiences like glamping under the stars or immersing yourself in rural life on a farm stay, you'll find the perfect haven to rest your head after a day of exploration.

Luxury Lodges:
Indulge in unparalleled luxury and immerse yourself in stunning surroundings at New Zealand's exclusive lodges. These intimate retreats offer exceptional service, gourmet cuisine, and curated experiences that showcase the best of the country's natural beauty and cultural heritage.

- **Helena Bay Lodge (Northland):** This secluded haven boasts private beaches, world-class cuisine, and personalized service for an unforgettable escape.
- **Huka Lodge (Taupo):** Nestled on the banks of the Waikato River, this iconic lodge offers luxurious suites, gourmet dining, and a range of outdoor activities.
- **Matakauri Lodge (Queenstown):** Experience alpine elegance with stunning views of Lake Wakatipu and the Remarkables mountain range. Enjoy fine dining, spa treatments, and personalized excursions.
- **Eagles Nest (Bay of Islands):** Perched atop a cliff overlooking the Bay of Islands, this exclusive retreat offers private villas with breathtaking views, private chefs, and tailored experiences.

Boutique Hotels:
Discover unique character and charm at New Zealand's boutique hotels. These stylish establishments offer personalized service, curated interiors, and a focus on local experiences, making them a popular choice for discerning travelers.
- **The George (Christchurch):** This elegant hotel blends classic architecture with modern amenities, offering a sophisticated stay in the heart of the Garden City.
- **Hotel Britomart (Auckland):** Experience urban luxury in this design-forward hotel, located in the vibrant Britomart precinct.
- **(Queenstown)**: Enjoy panoramic views of Lake Wakatipu and the Remarkables mountain range from this stylish hotel and apartment complex.
- **Hapuku Lodge + Tree Houses (Kaikoura):** Sleep amongst the treetops in unique tree houses, offering a unique blend of luxury and nature immersion.

Mid-Range Accommodations:

Find comfortable and convenient accommodations that offer value for money without sacrificing quality or amenities.

- **Motels:** These ubiquitous accommodations offer a range of room types, often with kitchenettes for self-catering. Look for motels with Qualmark ratings for quality assurance.
- **Apartments and Holiday Homes:** Ideal for families or groups, these self-contained units provide space, privacy, and the flexibility to cook your own meals.
- **Bed & Breakfasts (B&Bs):** Experience warm Kiwi hospitality and a homely atmosphere at B&Bs, often located in charming homes or heritage buildings.

Budget-Friendly Options:

New Zealand caters to budget-conscious travelers with a variety of affordable options that don't compromise on comfort or cleanliness.

- **Hostels:** Dormitory beds and private rooms are available at hostels throughout the country, offering a social atmosphere and opportunities to meet fellow travelers.
- **Holiday Parks and Campgrounds:** Pitch your tent or park your campervan at holiday parks and campgrounds, which offer basic amenities like showers, toilets, and laundry facilities. Some parks also have cabins for rent.
- **Backpacker Lodges:** These lodges provide a more intimate and communal experience than large hostels, often with shared kitchens and social areas.

Unique Stays:

Embrace the extraordinary with unique accommodation experiences that offer a taste of New Zealand's diverse landscapes and cultures..

- **Glamping:** Luxurious camping in stylish tents or yurts, often equipped with comfortable beds, private bathrooms, and outdoor soaking tubs.
- **Farm Stays:** Immerse yourself in rural life and experience authentic New Zealand hospitality on a working farm.
- **Historic Hotels:** Stay in a piece of history at one of New Zealand's heritage hotels, housed in grand buildings with period features.
- **Eco Retreats:** Choose from a range of eco-friendly accommodations that prioritize sustainability and minimize their environmental impact.

Recommendations for Different Budgets and Travel Styles:
- **Luxury Travelers:** Indulge in the opulence of Helena Bay Lodge, Huka Lodge, or Matakauri Lodge for an unforgettable experience.
- **Couples and Honeymooners**: Enjoy romantic retreats like Hapuku Lodge + Tree Houses or The Rees Hotel & Luxury Apartments for a special getaway.
- **Families:** Opt for spacious apartments or holiday homes for comfort and convenience, or embrace the outdoors with a campervan adventure.

- **Adventure Seekers:** Stay at hostels or backpacker lodges in adventure hubs like Queenstown or Taupo for a social atmosphere and easy access to activities.
- **Nature Lovers:** Choose eco retreats or glamping options in stunning natural settings like Abel Tasman National Park or Fiordland National Park.
- **Culture Vultures:** Experience Maori hospitality and learn about traditional customs with a farm stay or a night at a marae.

No matter your budget or travel style, New Zealand offers a wealth of accommodation options to ensure your stay is as memorable as your adventures. With a little research and planning, you can find the perfect haven to create lasting memories in this beautiful country.

Food and Drink: Where to find the best local cuisine and craft beverages

Embark on a culinary journey through New Zealand, where fresh, local ingredients, innovative techniques, and diverse cultural influences converge to create a vibrant and dynamic food scene. From bustling food markets to world-class restaurants, cozy cafés to craft breweries, this guide will lead you to the best places to savor the flavors of New Zealand.

Auckland:
Restaurants:
- **Depot Eatery & Oyster Bar:** Renowned for its fresh seafood and lively atmosphere, Depot is a must-visit for oyster lovers.
- **Orphans Kitchen:** A farm-to-table restaurant showcasing seasonal produce and creative dishes.
- **Kazuya:** Experience authentic Japanese cuisine with a focus on fresh, locally-sourced ingredients.

- **Sidart:** Indulge in fine dining with innovative tasting menus and impeccable service.

Cafés:
- **Best Ugly Bagels:** Savor delicious bagels with unique flavor combinations and creative toppings.
- **Little Bird Unbakery:** A haven for vegans and health-conscious eaters, offering raw, organic, and plant-based dishes.
- **Amano:** A stylish bakery and café serving artisanal bread, pastries, and coffee.

Bars:
- **Caretaker:** A hidden gem with a speakeasy vibe, serving expertly crafted cocktails and small plates.
- **The Jefferson:** A whisky lover's paradise with an extensive selection of whiskies from around the world.
- **Mea Culpa:** A lively bar with a focus on natural wines and craft beers.

Food Markets:
- **La Cigale French Market:** Immerse yourself in the flavors of France with fresh pastries, cheeses, cured meats, and other gourmet treats.
- **Auckland Night Markets:** Explore a variety of stalls offering international street food, crafts, and live music.

Wellington:
Restaurants:
- **Hiakai:** Celebrates Maori cuisine with a modern twist, showcasing native ingredients and traditional techniques.
- **Logan Brown:** A Wellington institution known for its sophisticated seasonal menu and elegant ambiance

- **Rita:** A cozy neighborhood bistro serving delicious tapas and sharing plates.

Cafés:
- **Customs Brew Bar:** A specialty coffee roaster and café with a focus on ethically sourced beans and expertly crafted brews.
- **Midnight Espresso:** A local favorite with a bohemian vibe, serving coffee, pastries, and light meals.

Bars:
- **Garage Project:** Visit the taproom of this innovative brewery to sample their unique and experimental beers.
- **Golding's Free Dive:** A popular bar with a lively atmosphere and a wide selection of local and international craft beers.

Food Markets:
- **Wellington Night Market:** Savor diverse international street food and local craft beer at this vibrant night market.
- **Harbourside Market:** Browse fresh produce, artisan foods, and crafts at this popular Sunday market.

Queenstown:
Restaurants:
- **Amisfield Bistro & Winery:** Experience farm-to-table dining with stunning views of Lake Hayes and the surrounding mountains.
- **Botswana Butchery:** A carnivore's dream, serving premium cuts of meat and a wide selection of wines.
- **Fergburger:** Join the queue for this iconic burger joint, known for its massive and delicious burgers.

Cafés:
- **Vudu Cafe & Larder:** A popular spot for coffee, brunch, and gourmet sandwiches.
- **Bespoke Kitchen:** A charming café with a focus on fresh, local ingredients and homemade baked goods.

Bars:
- **Little Blackwood:** A cozy cocktail bar with a creative menu and intimate atmosphere.
- **Atlas Beer Café:** Enjoy a wide selection of craft beers from around New Zealand and the world.

Christchurch:
Restaurants:
- **Pescatore:** A seafood lover's paradise, serving fresh and innovative dishes with stunning views of the Avon River.
- **Fiddlesticks Restaurant & Bar:** A vibrant establishment with a focus on modern New Zealand cuisine and local wines.
- **King of Snake:** Experience the flavors of Southeast Asia at this popular restaurant, known for its shared plates and lively atmosphere.

Cafés:

- **C1 Espresso:** A unique café housed in a historic post office building, serving coffee, pastries, and light meals.
- **The Caffeine Laboratory:** A specialty coffee roaster and café with a minimalist aesthetic and a focus on high-quality coffee.

Bars:

- **The Last Word:** A speakeasy-style whisky bar with a sophisticated atmosphere and extensive whisky selection.
- **Smash Palace:** A local institution with a quirky vibe, serving burgers, craft beers, and live music.

Beyond the Cities:

- **Food Trails:** Explore various food trails throughout the country, showcasing regional specialties and local producers.
- **Wine Tours:** Embark on a guided wine tour to discover New Zealand's renowned wine regions and sample their finest offerings.
- **Farm Stays and Cooking Classes:** Immerse yourself in the culinary culture by staying on a working farm and learning to cook traditional dishes.

No matter where your travels take you in New Zealand, you'll be greeted with a diverse and delicious culinary landscape. Embrace the opportunity to savor the flavors of this extraordinary country, and let your taste buds guide you on an unforgettable gastronomic adventure.

Shopping: Unique souvenirs, local crafts, and designer fashion

New Zealand's shopping scene is a delightful mix of unique treasures, local craftsmanship, and cutting-edge fashion. Whether you're seeking a special memento of your trip, a one-of-a-kind gift, or a stylish addition to your wardrobe, New Zealand's shops and markets offer a diverse range of options to satisfy every shopper's desires.

Unique Souvenirs:
Capture the essence of your New Zealand adventure with unique souvenirs that reflect the country's natural beauty, cultural heritage, and creative spirit.

- **Pounamu (Greenstone):** This precious stone holds deep cultural significance for Maori people and is often carved into intricate jewelry, pendants, and sculptures. Look for authentic pounamu pieces at reputable stores like Mountain Jade or The Jade Factory.
- **Bone Carvings:** Maori artisans create exquisite carvings from bone, often depicting traditional figures and symbols. These intricate pieces make for meaningful and treasured souvenirs.
- **Wood Carvings:** New Zealand's native timber is transformed into stunning carvings, from small figurines to large sculptures. Look for pieces crafted from kauri, totara, or rimu wood.
- **Woven Products:** Maori weaving techniques produce beautiful baskets, mats, and cloaks. Seek out traditional and contemporary woven pieces at local markets or art galleries.
- **Kiwiana:** Embrace the quirky side of New Zealand culture with kitschy Kiwiana souvenirs like Buzzy Bee toys, pineapple lumps (chocolate-covered pineapple candy), and sheepskin products.

New Zealand Travel Guide

- **Manuka Honey:** Renowned for its antibacterial properties and unique flavor, Manuka honey is a popular and delicious souvenir. Look for UMF (Unique Manuka Factor) certified honey for guaranteed quality.

Local Crafts:

Support local artisans and discover unique handcrafted items at New Zealand's craft markets, galleries, and shops.

- **The Arts Centre (Christchurch):** This historic complex houses a collection of art galleries, craft workshops, and boutique shops showcasing local talent.
- **Nelson Saturday Market:** Browse a wide range of locally made crafts, art, jewelry, clothing, and food at this vibrant weekly market.
- **Otago Farmers Market (Dunedin):** Held every Saturday morning, this bustling market offers fresh produce, artisan cheeses, baked goods, and handcrafted items.
- **The Tannery (Christchurch):** This eclectic shopping precinct features a mix of boutique stores, cafes, and restaurants, showcasing local designers and artisans.
- **Masterworks Gallery (Nelson):** Discover contemporary New Zealand art and crafts, including paintings, sculptures, ceramics, and glasswork.

Designer Fashion:

New Zealand has a burgeoning fashion scene, with talented designers creating unique and stylish clothing, footwear, and accessories.

- **Karen Walker:** This internationally renowned designer is known for her quirky yet sophisticated style, featuring bold prints, playful accessories, and iconic sunglasses.

- **Kate Sylvester:** Discover elegant and timeless womenswear with a focus on quality fabrics and impeccable tailoring.
- **Zambesi:** Explore avant-garde designs with a minimalist aesthetic, featuring monochromatic palettes and architectural silhouettes.
- **Kathryn Wilson:** Treat yourself to stylish footwear with a wide range of shoes, boots, and sandals crafted from premium materials.
- **WORLD:** This iconic New Zealand brand is known for its bold and eclectic designs, pushing the boundaries of fashion.

Shopping Districts and Markets:
Explore these vibrant shopping destinations for a mix of local and international brands, unique boutiques, and lively markets.

- **Queen Street (Auckland):** The main shopping street in Auckland, lined with department stores, international brands, and independent shops.
- **Britomart Precinct (Auckland):** A stylish and sophisticated area with high-end fashion boutiques, designer stores, and trendy cafes.

- **Lambton Quay (Wellington):** The bustling heart of Wellington's shopping district, featuring department stores, international brands, and independent shops.
- **The Crossing (Christchurch):** A modern shopping mall with a mix of international and local retailers, as well as a cinema and food court.

Individual Shops Worth Visiting:
- **Shut the Front Door (Wellington):** A quirky gift shop with a focus on local designers and unique products.
- **Iko Iko (Auckland):** A curated collection of sustainable and ethical fashion, homeware, and gifts.
- **Paper Plane Store (Wellington):** A haven for stationery lovers, featuring beautiful notebooks, pens, and other paper goods.
- **The Vault (Christchurch):** A multi-designer boutique showcasing contemporary New Zealand fashion and accessories.

Remember to inquire about the GST (Goods and Services Tax) refund scheme if you're a visitor to New Zealand. You may be eligible to claim a refund on the GST paid on goods purchased and exported from the country. By venturing into the vibrant shopping districts, browsing local markets, and supporting talented artisans and designers, you'll discover a world of unique treasures and stylish finds that will remind you of your unforgettable New Zealand adventure.

Festivals and Events: Experiencing the cultural vibrancy of New Zealand

New Zealand's calendar is filled with a diverse array of festivals and events that celebrate the country's unique culture, creativity, and natural beauty. From vibrant Maori cultural festivals to world-class sporting events, food and wine celebrations to arts and music extravaganzas, there's always something exciting happening in New Zealand. Immerse yourself in the festivities and experience the Kiwi spirit firsthand.

Summer Festivals and Events (December-February):
- **Rhythm and Vines (Gisborne):** This iconic music festival is held over New Year's Eve, making it the first place in the world to welcome the new year. Dance the night away to international and local acts while enjoying the stunning coastal setting.
- **WOMAD (New Plymouth):** The World of Music, Arts, and Dance festival showcases diverse musical performances from around the globe, celebrating cultural exchange and artistic expression.
- **Splore Festival (Auckland):** This multi-day music and arts festival features a vibrant mix of music genres, workshops, art installations, and a family-friendly atmosphere.
- **Lantern Festival (Auckland)**: Celebrate Chinese New Year with a dazzling display of lanterns, cultural performances, and delicious street food.
- **New Zealand International Arts Festival (Wellington):** This biennial festival showcases a diverse range of performing arts, including theater, dance, music, and visual arts from New Zealand and around the world.

Autumn Festivals and Events (March-May):

- **Hokitika Wildfoods Festival (Hokitika):** This quirky festival celebrates the wild side of New Zealand cuisine with a focus on unusual and exotic foods like huhu grubs, mountain oysters, and possum pie.
- **Warbirds Over Wanaka International Airshow (Wanaka):** Witness thrilling aerial displays of vintage aircraft, including World War II fighters and bombers.
- **Auckland Heritage Festival:** Delve into Auckland's rich history and heritage with a series of events, tours, and talks.
- **Hokitika Gorge Walk:** Experience the stunning beauty of the Hokitika Gorge, where the turquoise waters flow through a dramatic rock gorge. The autumn foliage adds a touch of magic to the scenery.

Winter Festivals and Events (June-August):

- **Queenstown Winter Festival (Queenstown):** A ten-day celebration of winter with a jam-packed schedule of events, including street parties, concerts, fireworks displays, and sporting competitions.
- **Matariki:** The Maori New Year, marked by the rising of the Pleiades star cluster. Celebrations often include feasts, storytelling, and cultural performances.
- **New Zealand International Film Festival:** This nationwide festival showcases a diverse selection of films from around the world, with screenings in major cities and regional centers.
- **Ruapehu's Mardi Gras (Ohakune):** A weekend of festivities celebrating the start of the ski season with live music, costume parties, and a torchlight parade down the slopes.

Spring Festivals and Events (September-November):
- **World of WearableArt (WOW) (Wellington):** This internationally renowned competition showcases wearable art creations that push the boundaries of fashion, art, and design.
- **Alexandra Blossom Festival (Alexandra):** Celebrate the arrival of spring with a vibrant parade, live music, food stalls, and the crowning of the Blossom Queen.
- **Sculpture on the Gulf (Waiheke Island):** A biennial exhibition of contemporary sculptures set against the stunning backdrop of Waiheke Island's coastal landscape.
- **Garden Festivals:** New Zealand's spring gardens are a sight to behold. Attend one of the many garden festivals, like the Ellerslie International Flower Show or the Taranaki Garden Spectacular, to admire colorful blooms and innovative garden designs.

Unique Maori Cultural Festivals:
- **Te Matatini:** The national kapa haka festival, showcasing the best Maori performing arts groups from around New Zealand.
- **Waitangi Day (February 6th):** Commemorates the signing of the Treaty of Waitangi with cultural performances, historical reenactments, and a festive atmosphere.
- **Pasifika Festival (Auckland):** Celebrates the diverse cultures of the Pacific Islands with traditional music, dance, food, and craft demonstrations.

Sporting Events:
- **Rugby Sevens Tournaments:** Experience the fast-paced action of rugby sevens at tournaments held throughout the country.
- **Cricket Matches:** Catch a game of cricket, New Zealand's national summer sport, at one of the many stadiums across the country.

- **The Coast to Coast**: A multi-sport race that traverses the South Island, testing athletes' endurance in kayaking, cycling, and running.

Tips for Attending Festivals and Events:
- **Book Accommodation in Advance:** Popular events often lead to high demand for accommodation, so book your stay well in advance.
- **Purchase Tickets Early**: Some festivals and events have limited ticket availability, so secure your tickets early to avoid disappointment.
- **Check Schedules and Locations:** Many festivals and events have multiple venues and activities spread out over several days. Check the schedule to plan your time accordingly.
- **Be Prepared for the Weather:** New Zealand's weather can be unpredictable, so be prepared for all conditions. Pack layers, sunscreen, a hat, and rain gear.
- **Respect Local Customs:** When attending cultural events, be respectful of local customs and traditions.

By immersing yourself in the vibrant festivals and events of New Zealand, you'll gain a deeper understanding of the country's unique culture, creativity, and passion for celebration. Let the rhythm of the music, the colors of the art, and the excitement of the sporting events leave a lasting impression on your New Zealand adventure.

Language and Etiquette: Understanding Kiwi slang and cultural norms

New Zealanders, often referred to as Kiwis, are known for their friendly and laid-back nature. However, like any culture, they have their own unique slang, customs, and social norms. Understanding these nuances will help you interact with locals respectfully and navigate social situations with ease.

Kiwi Slang:

Kiwis are fond of their slang, often shortening words or using colorful expressions. Here are some common terms you might encounter:

- **Sweet as:** Means "great" or "no problem."
- **Choice! or Chur (cheers)**: Used to express enthusiasm or agreement.
- **Kia ora:** A Maori greeting meaning "hello" or "good health."
- **Tiki tour:** A scenic detour or leisurely drive.
- **Bach (pronounced "batch"):** A holiday home or beach house.
- **Jandals:** Flip-flops or sandals.
- **Dairy:** A small convenience store.
- **Chilly bin:** A cooler or insulated box for keeping food and drinks cold.
- **Heaps:** A lot or many.
- **Ta:** Thank you (from Maori).

Cultural Norms:

- **Egalitarianism:** Kiwis value equality and informality. Avoid excessive displays of wealth or status, and address people by their first names.

- **Directness:** Kiwis tend to be direct and honest in their communication. Don't be offended if they offer constructive criticism; it's often meant to be helpful.
- **Humour:** Kiwis appreciate a good sense of humor, often using self-deprecating jokes. Don't take their teasing too seriously, and try to have a laugh along with them.
- **Outdoor Culture:** Kiwis love the outdoors, and activities like hiking, camping, and water sports are a big part of their lifestyle. Embrace the opportunity to join them in exploring the country's natural beauty.
- **Respect for the Environment:** Kiwis are passionate about protecting their environment. Be mindful of your impact by recycling, conserving water, and following responsible tourism practices.
- **Maori Culture**: Show respect for Maori culture by learning a few basic phrases, asking permission before taking photos at sacred sites, and removing your shoes before entering a marae (Maori meeting house).

Interacting with Locals:
- **Greet with a Smile:** Kiwis are friendly and approachable. Start a conversation with a smile and a simple "hello" or "kia ora."
- **Show Genuine Interest:** Ask questions about their culture, interests, or local recommendations. Kiwis appreciate genuine curiosity and are often happy to share their knowledge and experiences.
- **Offer a Helping Hand:** If you see someone in need of assistance, offer to help. Kiwis are known for their community spirit and willingness to lend a hand.
- **Respect Personal Space:** Kiwis value personal space, so avoid standing too close or touching someone without their permission.

- **Be Punctual:** Arriving on time for appointments and social gatherings is important in New Zealand.
- **Say "Thank You" and "Please":** Good manners are appreciated in any culture, and New Zealand is no exception. Use "please" when making requests and "thank you" to show appreciation.

Navigating Social Situations:
- **Gift Giving:** If you're invited to someone's home, it's customary to bring a small gift, such as a bottle of wine, flowers, or chocolates.
- **Shoes Off:** It's common practice to remove your shoes before entering someone's home. Look for a shoe rack or pile of shoes by the door, and follow suit.
- **BYO (Bring Your Own):** Some restaurants and events are BYO, meaning you can bring your own alcoholic beverages. Check with the establishment beforehand to confirm their BYO policy.
- **Tipping:** Tipping is not expected in New Zealand, but rounding up the bill or leaving a small amount for exceptional service is appreciated.
- **Table Manners:** Basic table manners are expected, such as using cutlery correctly and avoiding talking with your mouth full.
- **Conversation Starters:** Topics like sports (especially rugby), outdoor activities, travel, and local food and wine are usually safe and enjoyable conversation starters.

By understanding and respecting Kiwi slang, cultural norms, and social etiquette, you'll create meaningful connections with locals and enjoy a more immersive and rewarding experience in New Zealand. Remember, the key is to be open-minded, respectful, and willing to learn. Embrace the unique aspects of Kiwi culture, and you'll find yourself welcomed with open arms into this friendly and down-to-earth society.

Health and Safety: Tips for staying healthy and safe on your journey

New Zealand is a relatively safe and healthy destination, but it's important to be prepared and take precautions to ensure a smooth and enjoyable trip. By following these tips, you can minimize risks and maximize your well-being while exploring this beautiful country.

Before You Go:
- **Vaccinations:** No specific vaccinations are required for entry into New Zealand. However, it's recommended to be up-to-date on routine vaccinations, such as measles-mumps-rubella (MMR) and diphtheria-tetanus-pertussis (DTP). If you plan on participating in outdoor activities or visiting remote areas, consider vaccinations for hepatitis A, hepatitis B, and influenza. Consult your doctor for personalized advice based on your health history and itinerary.
- **Travel Insurance:** Obtaining comprehensive travel insurance is crucial for any trip to New Zealand.

- Make sure your policy covers medical expenses, emergency evacuation, trip cancellation, and loss or theft of belongings. It's also wise to check if your insurance covers adventure activities like bungy jumping or skiing, as these might require additional coverage.
- **Medications and First Aid:** Pack any prescription medications you need, along with a basic first aid kit containing essentials like pain relievers, antihistamines, antiseptic wipes, bandages, and insect repellent. If you have any specific medical conditions, carry a letter from your doctor outlining your condition and any necessary treatments.
- **Emergency Contacts:** Keep a list of emergency contacts handy, including the local emergency number (111), the contact information for your embassy or consulate, and the phone numbers of your travel companions and family members back home.

Health and Safety While Traveling:

- **Sun Protection**: New Zealand's UV radiation levels are high, so protect yourself from the sun by wearing sunscreen with a high SPF, a hat, sunglasses, and protective clothing. Seek shade during the hottest part of the day and stay hydrated by drinking plenty of water.
- **Water Safety:** New Zealand's beaches and waterways are beautiful but can also be dangerous. Always swim between the flags at patrolled beaches, be aware of strong currents and rips, and never swim alone. If you're planning water activities like kayaking or boating, wear a life jacket and check weather conditions before heading out.

- **Food and Water Safety:** Tap water is generally safe to drink throughout New Zealand. However, if you're in a remote area or unsure about the water source, it's best to boil or purify water before drinking. When dining out, choose reputable establishments and avoid raw or undercooked food, especially seafood.
- **Driving Safety:** If you're driving, always wear your seatbelt, adhere to speed limits, and avoid driving under the influence of alcohol or drugs. New Zealand's roads can be narrow and winding, so drive cautiously and be prepared for changing weather conditions. Familiarize yourself with local road rules and regulations before getting behind the wheel.
- **Outdoor Safety:** New Zealand's diverse landscapes offer endless opportunities for outdoor adventures. However, it's important to be prepared and take necessary precautions. Check weather forecasts before heading out, inform someone of your plans, and carry a map, compass, or GPS device. Pack appropriate clothing and gear for the activity and terrain, and be aware of potential hazards like changing weather conditions, slippery trails, and unpredictable wildlife.
- **Personal Safety:** While New Zealand is generally a safe country, it's always wise to be vigilant and aware of your surroundings. Avoid walking alone at night in unfamiliar areas, keep valuables out of sight, and use hotel safes when available. Trust your instincts and seek help if you feel unsafe.

Additional Tips:
- **Learn Basic First Aid:** Taking a basic first aid course can equip you with essential skills to handle minor injuries and emergencies.

- **Be Aware of Natural Hazards:** New Zealand is prone to earthquakes and volcanic activity. Familiarize yourself with evacuation procedures and emergency shelters in case of natural disasters.
- **Respect Wildlife:** Observe animals from a distance and avoid disturbing their natural behavior. Never feed wildlife, as it can alter their habits and create dependence on humans.
- **Travel Responsibly:** Minimize your impact on the environment by following sustainable practices like reducing waste, conserving water, and supporting local businesses.

By taking these precautions and staying informed, you can ensure a safe, healthy, and enjoyable trip to New Zealand. Remember, a little preparation goes a long way in ensuring a worry-free adventure.

Staying Connected: Internet access and mobile phone tips

Staying connected while traveling in New Zealand is easier than ever, with various options available to access the internet, make calls, and stay in touch with loved ones. Whether you're a digital nomad working on the go, a social media enthusiast sharing your adventures, or simply want to stay connected for practical purposes, New Zealand has you covered.

Internet Access:
- **Wi-Fi:** Free Wi-Fi is widely available throughout New Zealand, especially in urban areas. Cafés, restaurants, hotels, and libraries often offer complimentary Wi-Fi for customers and guests.

You can also find public Wi-Fi hotspots in many city centers, parks, and transport hubs. However, be cautious when using public Wi-Fi and avoid accessing sensitive information, as these networks may not be secure.

- **Mobile Data:** Purchasing a local SIM card with a data plan is a convenient and cost-effective option for staying connected on the go. Major mobile carriers like Spark, Vodafone, and 2degrees offer prepaid SIM cards with various data packages to suit your needs and budget. You can purchase these SIM cards at airports, convenience stores, and mobile phone shops.
- **Pocket Wi-Fi:** Renting a pocket Wi-Fi device is another option for staying connected, especially if you're traveling with multiple devices or prefer to have your own secure network. Several companies offer pocket Wi-Fi rentals, allowing you to connect multiple devices to the internet simultaneously.

Mobile Phone Plans:
- **Prepaid Plans:** Prepaid plans are a popular choice for travelers as they offer flexibility and control over your spending. You can easily top up your credit online or at retail outlets.
- **Monthly Plans**: If you're staying in New Zealand for an extended period, consider a monthly plan. These plans often offer more data and additional benefits like free calls and texts.
- **Roaming:** If you prefer to use your home SIM card, check with your provider about their international roaming rates for New Zealand. Roaming can be expensive, so it's often more cost-effective to purchase a local SIM card.

Other Ways to Stay Connected:

- **Internet Cafes:** While less common than they once were, internet cafes can still be found in some towns and cities, offering an option for those without a smartphone or laptop.
- **Libraries:** Many public libraries offer free Wi-Fi and computer access for visitors.
- **Accommodation:** Most hotels, motels, and hostels provide free Wi-Fi for guests.

Tips for Staying Connected:
- **Plan Ahead:** Research the different options available and choose the one that best suits your needs and budget.
- **Purchase a Local SIM Card:** This is often the most cost-effective and convenient way to stay connected with data and calls.
- **Compare Data Plans:** Compare different data plans from various mobile carriers to find the best deal for your usage.
- **Use Wi-Fi Whenever Possible:** Take advantage of free Wi-Fi in hotels, cafes, and public spaces to conserve your mobile data.
- **Download Offline Maps:** Offline maps can be a lifesaver if you lose signal or run out of data. Download maps of the areas you'll be visiting before you go.
- **Use Messaging Apps:** Apps like WhatsApp, Facebook Messenger, and Viber allow you to communicate with friends and family for free over Wi-Fi.

These are just a few examples, and plans can change, so it's always best to check the latest offers from each carrier.

Staying Connected Safely:
- **Use Strong Passwords:** Protect your online accounts with strong, unique passwords.
- **Be Wary of Public Wi-Fi:** Avoid accessing sensitive information like bank accounts or credit cards on public Wi-Fi networks.
- **Install Security Software:** Use antivirus and anti-malware software on your devices.
- **Keep Your Devices Updated**: Install the latest software updates to protect against security vulnerabilities.
- **Be Mindful of What You Share:** Avoid sharing personal information online or with strangers.

By following these tips and utilizing the various options available, you can stay connected in New Zealand while exploring this beautiful country. Whether you're checking emails, uploading photos, or calling loved ones back home, staying connected will enhance your travel experience and keep you informed and in touch.

Chapter 5

Additional Resources

Useful Phrases in Te Reo Māori (Maori language)

Learning a few basic phrases in Te Reo Māori, the language of New Zealand's indigenous people, is a wonderful way to show respect and connect with the local culture. Here's a list of common phrases and greetings, along with pronunciation guides and cultural context:

Greetings:
- **Kia ora:** (kee-o-ra) Hello/Good health. This versatile greeting can be used in formal and informal settings.
- **Tēnā koe:** (teh-nah kweh) Hello (to one person, formal). Use this when addressing someone you don't know well or in a formal setting.
- **Tēnā kōrua:** (teh-nah koh-roo-ah) Hello (to two people, formal).

- **Ata mārie:** (ah-tah mah-ree-eh) Good morning (more formal).
- **Kia ora kōtōu:** (kee-o-ra koh-toh) Hello everyone (informal).
- **Nau mai, haere mai:** (noh-my hi-reh-my) Welcome. This warm welcome is often used to greet visitors.

Farewells:
- **Ka kite anō:** (kah kee-teh ah-noh) See you again (informal).
- **E noho rā:** (eh no-hoh rah) Goodbye (said by the person leaving).
- **Haere rā:** (ha-eh-reh rah) Goodbye (said by the person staying).
- **Mā te wā:** (mah teh wah) See you later.

Other Useful Phrases:
- **Kei te pēhea koe?:** (kay teh pay-ah ko-eh) How are you? (to one person)
- **Kei te pai:** (kay teh pie) I'm fine/good.
- **Tino pai:** (tee-noh pie) Very good.
- **Ngā mihi:** (nah me-he) Thanks.
- **Ngā mihi nui:** (nah me-he noo-ee) Thank you very much.
- **Aroha:** (ah-roh-hah) Love, compassion, empathy. This word expresses a deep connection and affection.
- **Manaakitanga:** (mah-nah-kee-tah-nah) Hospitality, kindness, generosity.
- **Tūrangawaewae:** (too-rah-nga-why-why) A place to stand, a sense of belonging. This concept emphasizes the importance of connection to the land and community.
- **Whakapapa:** (fah-kah-pah-pah) Genealogy, lineage, connection. This concept underscores the importance of ancestry and interconnectedness in Maori culture.

Pronunciation Tips:
Vowels are pronounced as in Spanish or Italian. "Wh" is pronounced as "f," "ng" as in "sing," and "r" as a rolled "r." Stress is usually on the first syllable of each word.

Cultural Context:
- **Respect:** Te Reo Māori is a taonga (treasure) for the Maori people. Approach the language with respect and humility.
- **Pronunciation:** Try your best to pronounce words correctly, but don't be afraid to ask for help or clarification.
- **Context:** Consider the setting and relationship when using greetings. "Tēnā koe" is more formal than "Kia ora."
- **Reciprocity:** If someone greets you in Te Reo Māori, try to respond in kind, even if it's just with "kia ora."

By incorporating these phrases into your interactions, you can show your appreciation for Maori culture and connect with locals in a more meaningful way.

Packing Checklist

New Zealand's diverse climate and range of activities require thoughtful packing. Here are comprehensive packing lists tailored to different types of travelers and seasons, ensuring you're prepared for any adventure:

Essentials for All Travelers:
- Passport and Visa (if required)
- Travel Insurance Documents
- Credit/Debit Cards and Cash
- Adapters and Converters: New Zealand uses Type I plugs (2 flat pins and a grounding pin).

- Medications and First Aid Kit
- Reusable Water Bottle
- **Sunscreen and Sunglasses:** Even in winter, the sun can be strong, especially at higher altitudes.
- **Insect Repellent**: Protect yourself from sandflies, particularly in warmer months and the South Island's West Coast.
- Travel Journal and Pen
- Camera or Smartphone
- Portable Charger

Clothing:
- **Base Layers (2-3)**: Merino wool or synthetic fabrics are ideal for moisture-wicking and warmth.
- **T-shirts/Shirts (3-5):** Pack a mix of short-sleeved and long-sleeved options.
- **Sweaters/Fleeces (2-3):** Choose versatile layers for warmth.
- **Jacket (1):** A waterproof and windproof jacket is essential year-round.
- **Pants (2-3):** Pack comfortable pants or shorts for warmer weather and hiking pants for outdoor activities.
- **Underwear and Socks (7+):** Pack enough for your trip, considering laundry options.
- **Shoes (2-3 pairs):** Comfortable walking shoes or hiking boots, sandals or flip-flops for warmer weather, and a pair of dressier shoes for evenings out.

Seasonal Additions:
Summer (December-February):
- **Hat (wide-brimmed):** For sun protection.
- **Swimsuit:** For swimming and beach days.
- **Beach Towel:** If planning to visit beaches.

Autumn (March-May):
- **Light Scarf:** For added warmth on cooler evenings.
- **Waterproof Pants:** In case of rain.

Winter (June-August):
- **Thermal Underwear (2-3 sets):** For extra warmth in cold weather.
- **Warm Hat and Gloves:** Essential for snow activities or chilly evenings.
- **Thick Socks:** Merino wool is best for warmth and moisture-wicking.

Spring (September-November):
- **Layers:** Pack a variety of layers to adapt to changing temperatures.
- **Umbrella or Rain Jacket:** For frequent spring showers.

Activity-Specific Gear:
Hiking:
- **Hiking Boots (broken in):** Choose sturdy boots with good ankle support.
- **Daypack:** Carry water, snacks, extra layers, a first-aid kit, and a headlamp.
- **Trekking Poles (optional):** Helpful for steep or challenging terrain.

Water Sports:
- **Rash Guard or Wetsuit:** For protection from the sun and cold water.
- **Water Shoes:** For rocky beaches or water activities.
- **Dry Bag:** Keep valuables safe and dry.

Skiing/Snowboarding:
- **Ski/Snowboard Gear:** Jacket, pants, goggles, gloves, and thermal layers.
- **Helmet:** Safety first!

Camping:
- Tent, Sleeping Bag, and Sleeping Pad: Choose gear appropriate for the season and expected temperatures.
- Cooking Equipment (if needed): Compact stove, cookware, utensils.
- Headlamp or Flashlight: For navigating around the campsite at night.

Packing Tips for Different Travelers:
- **Backpackers:** Pack light and prioritize versatile clothing that can be mixed and matched. Use packing cubes to organize your gear and compress clothing.
- **Luxury Travelers:** Consider a larger suitcase for extra outfits and accessories. Pack a few dressier options for evenings out.
- **Families:** Pack extra clothes and snacks for children. Consider a stroller or baby carrier if traveling with infants or toddlers.
- **Adventure Seekers:** Focus on durable and functional clothing and gear suitable for outdoor activities. Bring a first aid kit, headlamp, and other essential safety items.

By packing strategically and considering your specific needs and activities, you'll be well-prepared to enjoy all that New Zealand has to offer, no matter your travel style or the season.

Emergency Contacts

Emergency Services:
- **111:** This is the nationwide emergency number for Police, Fire, and Ambulance services. It's a free call from any phone, including mobile phones with no credit.

Medical Facilities:
- **Hospitals**: Each major city and town has a public hospital with emergency departments. Some private hospitals also offer emergency services.
- **Medical Centres and GP Clinics:** These are available throughout the country for non-emergency medical care.
- **Pharmacies:** For prescription and over-the-counter medications.
- **Healthline:** 0800 611 116 (free call within New Zealand) for confidential health advice from registered nurses.

Police:
- **105**: This is the non-emergency number to report a crime or get police assistance.
- **Local Police Stations:** Police stations are located in most towns and cities.

Roadside Assistance:
- **AA (Automobile Association):** 0800 500 222 or *222 from your mobile phone.
- **Other Providers:** Some car rental companies offer their own roadside assistance services.

Embassies and Consulates:
- **Your Country's Embassy/Consulate:** Contact your embassy or consulate for assistance with lost or stolen passports, legal issues, or other emergencies. You can find a list of embassies and consulates in New Zealand on the New Zealand Ministry of Foreign Affairs and Trade website: https://www.mfat.govt.nz/en/

Other Relevant Organizations:
- **Citizens Advice Bureau (CAB):** Free and confidential advice on a range of issues, including legal, financial, and consumer matters.
- **Department of Conservation (DOC):** Information and assistance regarding national parks, conservation areas, and outdoor activities.
- **i-SITE Visitor Information Centres:** Located throughout New Zealand, i-SITE centers provide travel information, maps, brochures, and booking services.

Additional Tips:
- **Save Emergency Contacts:** Store these important phone numbers in your phone and carry a printed copy in case your phone battery dies or you lose signal.
- **Register with Your Embassy:** If you're a foreign visitor, register your travel plans with your embassy or consulate. This will make it easier for them to contact you in case of an emergency.
- **Know Your Location:** When hiking or traveling in remote areas, always let someone know your itinerary and expected return time.

New Zealand Travel Guide

New Zealand Travel Apps and Websites

Navigating and planning your New Zealand journey is made easier with a variety of helpful apps and websites designed to enhance your travel experience. From finding the perfect accommodation and tracking weather conditions to navigating public transportation and discovering local gems, these digital tools are essential companions for any modern explorer.

Transportation:
- **Google Maps:** A reliable navigation app for driving, walking, and public transportation directions. It also provides real-time traffic updates and estimated travel times.
- **Apple Maps:** Another comprehensive mapping app with turn-by-turn navigation and information on points of interest.
- **Metlink (Wellington):** The official app for Wellington's public transport system, allowing you to plan journeys, check timetables, and purchase tickets.
- **AT Metro (Auckland):** The equivalent app for Auckland's public transport network.
- **InterCity:** The official app for InterCity buses, allowing you to book tickets and track your journeys.
- **Gaspy:** A handy app for finding the cheapest petrol (gasoline) prices near you.

Accommodation:
- **Booking.com:** A popular platform for booking hotels, apartments, and other accommodations. Offers a wide range of options and user reviews.
- **Airbnb:** Find unique stays, from private rooms to entire homes, hosted by locals.

New Zealand Travel Guide

- **Hostelworld:** A comprehensive resource for finding and booking hostels throughout New Zealand.
- **CamperMate:** An essential app for campervan travelers, providing information on campsites, dump stations, and other facilities.
- **Rankers Camping NZ:** Another useful app for finding camping spots, including both paid and free options.

Weather:
- **MetService:** The official weather app for New Zealand, providing accurate forecasts, warnings, and detailed information on rainfall, wind, and temperature.
- **WeatherWatch:** A popular alternative weather app with detailed forecasts and live weather radar.
- **NIWA** (National Institute of Water and Atmospheric Research): Provides comprehensive weather and climate information for New Zealand.

Local Information and Activities:
- **NZ Pocket Guide:** A comprehensive guide to New Zealand's attractions, activities, and local businesses.
- **Bookme:** Find and book discounted activities, tours, and attractions throughout the country.
- **Tripadvisor:** Read reviews and get recommendations for restaurants, attractions, and activities from fellow travelers.
- **The Spinoff:** A popular online magazine featuring news, commentary, and cultural insights about New Zealand.
- **Stuff:** A major news website covering a wide range of topics, including travel, events, and local news.

Maps (High-quality, detailed maps of North and South Island, major cities, and popular regions)

Auckland, New Zealand

SCAN THE QR CODE

1. open your device's camera app
2. point the camera at the QR code
3. Ensure the QR code is within the frame and well-lit
4. Wait for your device to recognize the QR code
5. Once recognized, tap on the map and input your current location for direction and distance to the destination

New Zealand Travel Guide

Wellington, New Zealand

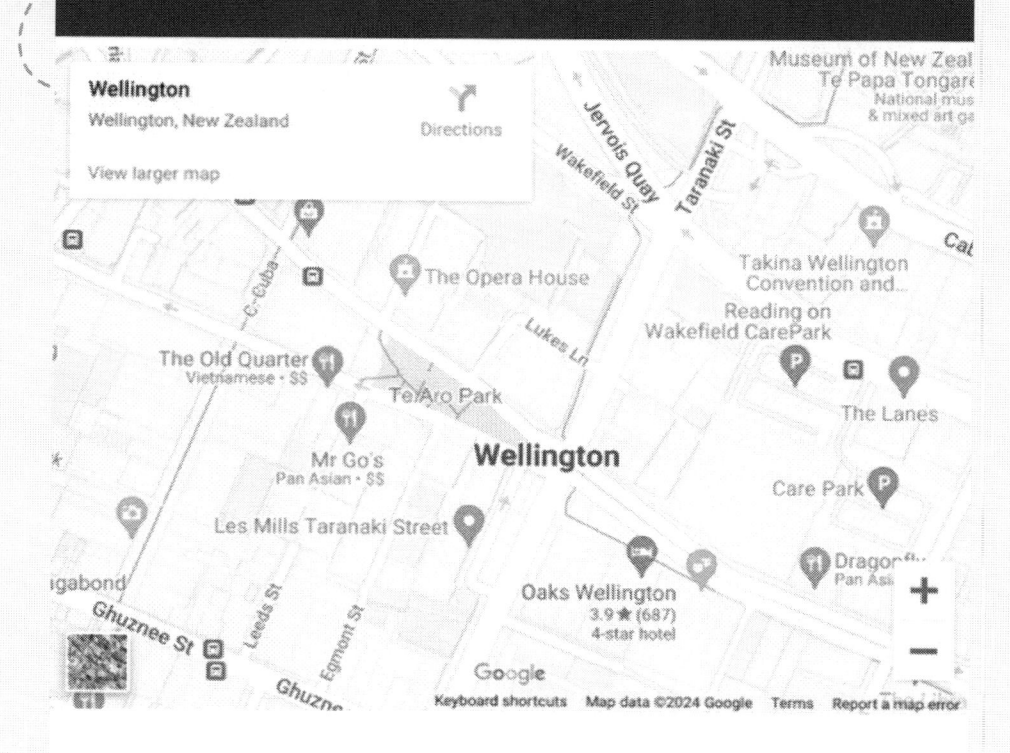

SCAN THE QR CODE

1. open your device's camera app
2. point the camera at the QR code
3. Ensure the QR code is within the frame and well-lit
4. Wait for your device to recognize the QR code
5. Once recognized, tap on the map and input your current location for direction and distance to the destination

New Zealand Travel Guide

Christchurch, New Zealand

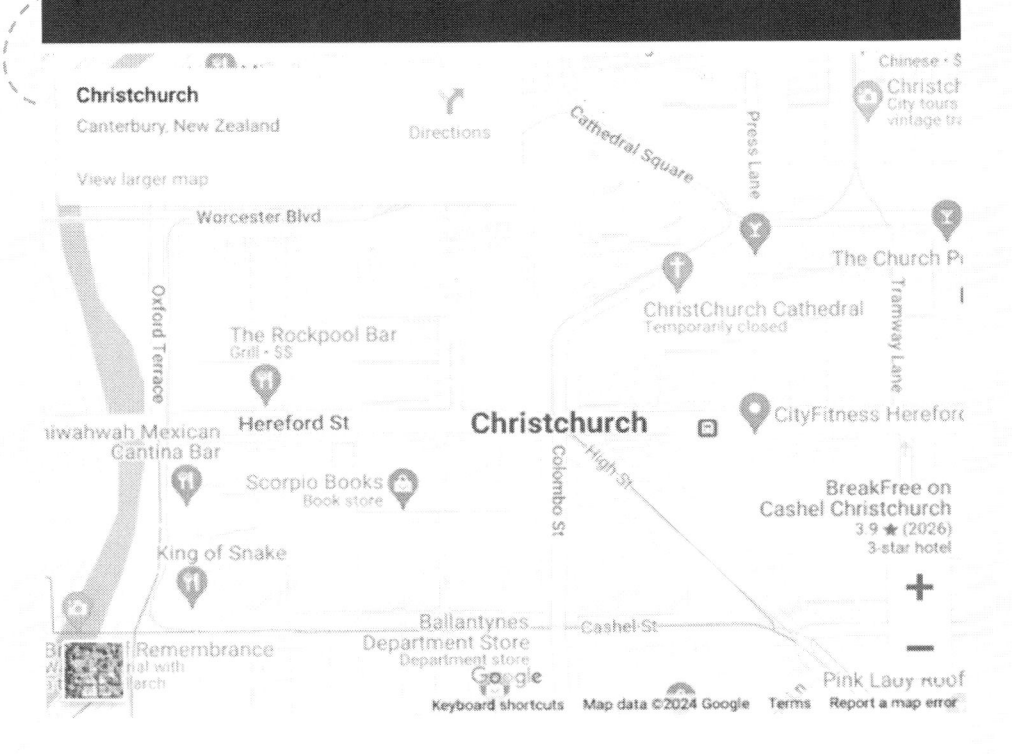

SCAN THE QR CODE

1. open your device's camera app
2. point the camera at the QR code
3. Ensure the QR code is within the frame and well-lit
4. Wait for your device to recognize the QR code
5. Once recognized, tap on the map and input your current location for direction and distance to the destination

New Zealand Travel Guide

Queenstown, New Zealand

SCAN THE QR CODE

1. open your device's camera app
2. point the camera at the QR code
3. Ensure the QR code is within the frame and well-lit
4. Wait for your device to recognize the QR code
5. Once recognized, tap on the map and input your current location for direction and distance to the destination

New Zealand Travel Guide

Milford Sound / Piopiotahi, Southland, New Zealand

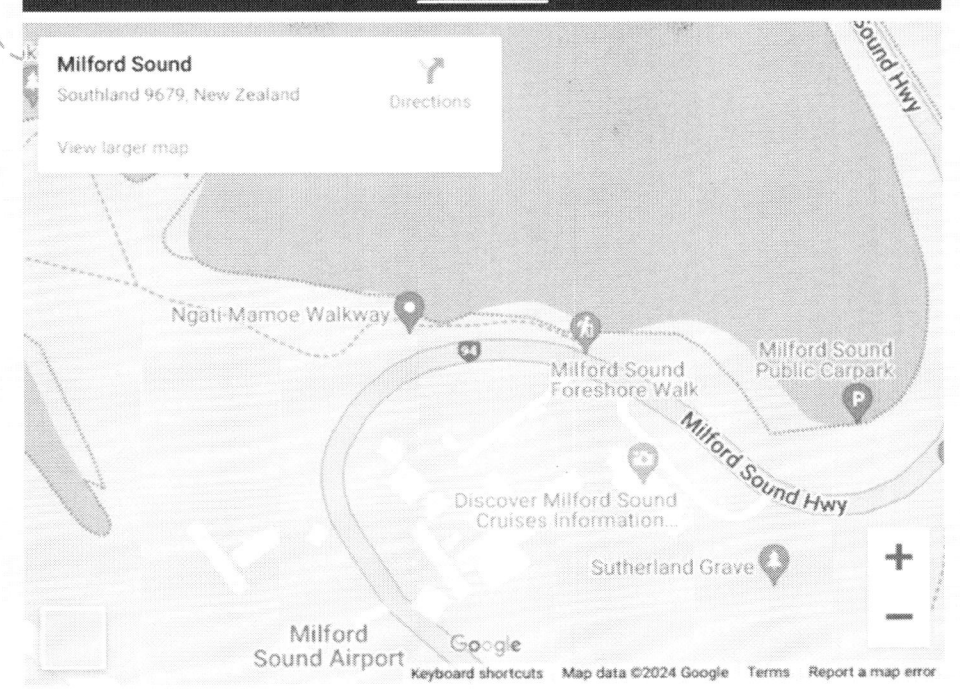

Milford Sound
Southland 9679, New Zealand
Directions
View larger map

SCAN THE QR CODE

1. open your device's camera app
2. point the camera at the QR code
3. Ensure the QR code is within the frame and well-lit
4. Wait for your device to recognize the QR code
5. Once recognized, tap on the map and input your current location for direction and distance to the destination

New Zealand Travel Guide

Franz Josef Glacier, West Coast 7886, New Zealand

Franz Josef Glacier
West Coast 7886, New Zealand
4.6 ★★★★★ 371 reviews
View larger map
Directions

Franz Josef Glacier
Sizable glacier viewed by guided tours

Google
Keyboard shortcuts   Map data ©2024   Terms   Report a map error

SCAN THE QR CODE

1. open your device's camera app
2. point the camera at the QR code
3. Ensure the QR code is within the frame and well-lit
4. Wait for your device to recognize the QR code
5. Once recognized, tap on the map and input your current location for direction and distance to the destination

New Zealand Travel Guide

Waiheke Island, Auckland, New Zealand

Waiheke Island
Auckland, New Zealand
4.7 ★★★★★ 445 reviews
View larger map

Directions

Waiheke Rd

Waiheke Island

Google
Keyboard shortcuts Map data ©2024 Google Terms Report a map error

SCAN THE QR CODE

1. open your device's camera app
2. point the camera at the QR code
3. Ensure the QR code is within the frame and well-lit
4. Wait for your device to recognize the QR code
5. Once recognized, tap on the map and input your current location for direction and distance to the destination

Waitomo Caves, New Zealand

SCAN THE QR CODE

1. open your device's camera app
2. point the camera at the QR code
3. Ensure the QR code is within the frame and well-lit
4. Wait for your device to recognize the QR code
5. Once recognized, tap on the map and input your current location for direction and distance to the destination

New Zealand Travel Guide 142

Tongariro National Park, New Zealand

Tongariro National Park
Manawatū-Whanganui 4691, New Zealand
4.8 ★★★★★ 5,700 reviews
View larger map

Directions

Tongariro National Park

Google
Keyboard shortcuts   Map data ©2024   Terms   Report a map error

SCAN THE QR CODE

1. open your device's camera app
2. point the camera at the QR code
3. Ensure the QR code is within the frame and well-lit
4. Wait for your device to recognize the QR code
5. Once recognized, tap on the map and input your current location for direction and distance to the destination

New Zealand Travel Guide

Abel Tasman National Park, New Zealand

Abel Tasman National Park
South Island 7183, New Zealand

Directions

4.8 ★★★★★ 1,941 reviews

View larger map

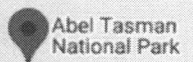

Abel Tasman National Park

Keyboard shortcuts   Map data ©2024   Terms   Report a map error

SCAN THE QR CODE

1. open your device's camera app
2. point the camera at the QR code
3. Ensure the QR code is within the frame and well-lit
4. Wait for your device to recognize the QR code
5. Once recognized, tap on the map and input your current location for direction and distance to the destination

New Zealand Travel Guide

Enhance your journey with interactive maps

Scan the QR codes on the maps throughout this guide to unlock a wealth of additional information, including:

- Interactive maps: Zoom in on specific regions and attractions for detailed navigation and exploration.
- Real-time updates: Get the latest information on weather conditions, road closures, and events happening near you.
- Exclusive content: Access bonus travel tips, insider recommendations, and hidden gems not found in the book.
-

To scan QR codes, simply download a free QR code reader app on your smartphone. We recommend using a reliable and user-friendly app such as:

- **QR CODE SCANNER & SCANNER APP** : AVAILABLE FOR BOTH IOS AND ANDROID DEVICES, THIS APP IS QUICK, EFFICIENT, AND OFFERS A SEAMLESS SCANNING EXPERIENCE.

By utilizing these interactive maps and QR codes, you can further personalize your New Zealand adventure and discover even more of what this beautiful country has to offer. Happy travels!

Kia Ora and Thank You!

As you embark on your New Zealand adventure armed with the knowledge and insights from this guide, I extend my heartfelt gratitude for choosing "New Zealand Travel Guide 2024: Your Ultimate Companion for Exploring the Land of the Long White Cloud" as your trusted companion. I hope this guide has inspired you to discover the wonders of Aotearoa, from its majestic landscapes and vibrant culture to its warm hospitality and thrilling adventures. It has been a privilege to share my passion for this extraordinary country with you.

As you create your own unforgettable memories in New Zealand, I would be honored if you would consider sharing your experience with fellow travelers. Your feedback is invaluable in helping me refine and improve future editions of this guide. If you have a moment, please leave a review on Amazon. Your stories and insights will not only help other travelers plan their own journeys but also contribute to the ongoing celebration of New Zealand's unique magic.

Thank you once again for choosing this guide, and may your adventures in the Land of the Long White Cloud be filled with joy, discovery, and wonder.

Ngā mihi nui,
Tony Mark

MY TRAVEL PLAN

TRAVEL ITINERARY

Date: _____

S S M T W T F

Date:

Location:

Budget:

Trip To-do List

Daily Expenses

Daily Log

- 6 AM
- 7 AM
- 8 AM
- 9 AM
- 10 AM
- 11 AM
- 12 PM
- 1 PM
- 2 PM
- 3 PM
- 4 PM
- 5 PM
- 6 PM
- 7 PM
- 8 PM

NOTE:

MY PACKING LIST

TRAVEL ITINERARY

Date: _____

S S M T W T F

THINGS TO PACK ✓

ACCOMODATION

Name of Hotel

Location:

Check In Date:

Check Out Date:

Total Cost:

TRANSPORT

NOTES

148

PLACES TO VISIT
TRAVEL ITINERARY

Date: _____

S S M T W T F

Place	Visitor's Review	✓
	☆☆☆☆☆☆☆☆☆☆	○
	☆☆☆☆☆☆☆☆☆☆	○
	☆☆☆☆☆☆☆☆☆☆	○
	☆☆☆☆☆☆☆☆☆☆	○
	☆☆☆☆☆☆☆☆☆☆	○
	☆☆☆☆☆☆☆☆☆☆	○
	☆☆☆☆☆☆☆☆☆☆	○
	☆☆☆☆☆☆☆☆☆☆	○
	☆☆☆☆☆☆☆☆☆☆	○
	☆☆☆☆☆☆☆☆☆☆	○
	☆☆☆☆☆☆☆☆☆☆	○
	☆☆☆☆☆☆☆☆☆☆	○
	☆☆☆☆☆☆☆☆☆☆	○
	☆☆☆☆☆☆☆☆☆☆	○

Notes

TRAVEL JOURNAL
TRAVEL REVIEW

Date: _____

S S M T W T F

Today's experience

Travel Checklist

DATE: _____
DESTINATION: _____

CLOTHES

- [ ] _____
- [ ] _____
- [ ] _____
- [ ] _____
- [ ] _____
- [ ] _____
- [ ] _____
- [ ] _____
- [ ] _____
- [ ] _____
- [ ] _____
- [ ] _____
- [ ] _____

BASICS

- [ ] _____
- [ ] _____
- [ ] _____
- [ ] _____
- [ ] _____
- [ ] _____

SHOES

- [ ] _____
- [ ] _____
- [ ] _____
- [ ] _____
- [ ] _____

TOILETRIES

- [ ] _____
- [ ] _____
- [ ] _____
- [ ] _____
- [ ] _____
- [ ] _____
- [ ] _____
- [ ] _____
- [ ] _____
- [ ] _____
- [ ] _____

ELECTRONICS

- [ ] _____
- [ ] _____
- [ ] _____
- [ ] _____
- [ ] _____
- [ ] _____
- [ ] _____
- [ ] _____

ACCESSORIES

- [ ] _____
- [ ] _____
- [ ] _____
- [ ] _____
- [ ] _____
- [ ] _____
- [ ] _____
- [ ] _____

OTHER

- [ ] _____
- [ ] _____
- [ ] _____

Important

- [ ] _____
- [ ] _____
- [ ] _____
- [ ] _____

Made in the USA
Columbia, SC
15 October 2024